PERGAMON INTERNATIONAL LIBRARY
of Science, Technology, Engineering and Social Studies
*The 1000-volume original paperback library in aid of education,
industrial training and the enjoyment of leisure*
Publisher: Robert Maxwell, M.C.

Twelve Little Housemates

D0775139

THE PERGAMON TEXTBOOK
INSPECTION COPY SERVICE

An inspection copy of any book published in the Pergamon International Library will gladly
be sent to academic staff without obligation for their consideration for course adoption or
recommendation. Copies may be retained for a period of 60 days from receipt and returned
if not suitable. When a particular title is adopted or recommended for adoption for class use
and the recommendation results in a sale of 12 or more copies, the inspection copy may
be retained with our compliments. The Publishers will be pleased to receive suggestions for
revised editions and new titles to be published in this important International Library.

Related Titles of Interest:

BRADBURY: The Microscope Past and Present

DUNCAN & WESTON-SMITH: The Encyclopaedia of Ignorance

HALL: Radiation and Life

CLEGG: General Science: Biology

Twelve Little Housemates

Enlarged and Revised Edition of the
Popular Book Describing Insects That
Live in Our Homes

BY

KARL VON FRISCH
Nobel Laureate

*Translated by A. T. Sugar,
formerly of the BBC Monitoring Service*

PERGAMON PRESS

OXFORD · NEW YORK · TORONTO · SYDNEY · PARIS · FRANKFURT

U.K.	Pergamon Press Ltd., Headington Hill Hall, Oxford OX3 0BW, England
U.S.A.	Pergamon Press Inc., Maxwell House, Fairview Park, Elmsford, New York 10523, U.S.A.
CANADA	Pergamon of Canada Ltd., 75 The East Mall, Toronto, Ontario, Canada
AUSTRALIA	Pergamon Press (Aust.) Pty. Ltd., 19a Boundary Street, Rushcutters Bay, N.S.W. 2011, Australia
FRANCE	Pergamon Press SARL, 24 rue des Ecoles, 75240 Paris, Cedex 05, France
FEDERAL REPUBLIC OF GERMANY	Pergamon Press GmbH, 6242 Kronberg-Taunus, Pferdstrasse 1, Federal Republic of Germany

Fourth German edition copyright © 1955 ZEHN KLEINE HAUSGENOSSEN published by Ernst Heimeran Verlag
English edition translation copyright © 1960 TEN LITTLE HOUSEMATES published by Pergamon Press Ltd. Reprinted 1964, 1969

German edition copyright © 1976 ZWÖLF KLEINE HAUSGENOSSEN published by Rowohlt Taschenbuch Verlag GmbH
Revised English edition translation copyright © 1978 TWELVE LITTLE HOUSEMATES published by Pergamon Press Ltd.

All Rights Reserved. No part of this publication may be reproduced, stored in a retrieval system or transmitted in any form or by any means: electronic, electrostatic, magnetic tape, mechanical, photocopying, recording or otherwise, without permission in writing from the publishers

British Library Cataloguing in Publication Data

Frisch, Karl von
Twelve little housemates.—Enlarged
and revised ed.—(Pergamon international library).
1. Insects 2. Household pests
I. Title II. Ten little housemates
595.7   QL463   78-40341
ISBN 0-08-021959-4 Hardcover
ISBN 0-08-021958-6 Flexicover

This translation is based on a translation by Margaret D. Senft from the fourth edition (1955) of the book ZEHN KLEINE HAUSGENOSSEN published in Munich by Ernst Heimeran Verlag

Printed in Great Britain by Biddles Ltd., Guildford, Surrey

Contents

Metric measurements have not been converted in this translation. For the convenience of those who are not familiar with the metric system, the following approximate equivalents are given:

1 kilometre (km) =1000 metres = $\frac{5}{8}$ mile

1 metre (m) =100 centimetres = $3\frac{1}{3}$ feet

1 centimetre (cm) =10 millimetres = $\frac{2}{5}$ inch

1 millimetre (mm) = $\frac{1}{25}$ inch

Acknowledgements

Figures on pages 9, 24, 79, 88, 99, 109, 113, 119, 126, 142 by Hans Pfletschinger; on pages 16, 59, 138 by Prof. Dr. Max Renner; on page 95 (top) by Dr. Thomas Heinzeller; on pages 87, 91, 93, 96 (top), 101, 103, 105, 106 by Christian Schuk; on pages 95 (bottom), 96 (bottom), 107 drawn from material by Jacobs/Renner; on pages 27, 31, 33, 35, 44, 55, 85, 117, 122 (top) by courtesy of Rowohlt-Archiv.

All other drawings by Dr. Richard Ehrlich and Walther Soellner.

Cover design by Benny Kandler.

The House-fly

A weary man has settled down for a well-earned nap after his midday meal on a hot summer day. All around is peace and quiet and his thoughts are just drifting over the frontier of dreamland when a house-fly, after cruising several times round the room, feels that the only place where it could possibly relax is on the man's forehead. It neither bites nor stings, but it tickles. Too nimble to allow itself to be caught and too silly to learn from experience that the human face is not the best air-strip, such a fly can drive all but the most placid to distraction. No, there's no doubt about it—the house-fly is a troublesome creature!

If, on the other hand, this happens after the first winter snow has fallen, the man will probably not be so cross. For at heart he is interested in all life. Outside, trees and plants lie dormant. Most of the lively birds have disappeared. Not such stay-at-homes as we, they are now enjoying life under sunny blue skies, while the butterflies and all the tiny creatures that populate the air in summer seem to have died. We almost welcome the sight and the sound of a fly in our room. It's no longer a "troublesome creature", not even a nuisance. We are inclined to look at it as one of Nature's handiworks and to wonder if there is not something attractive about it after all.

Everyone must admit that the fly is a trim little creature. And it does seem to set store by cleanliness; at least it doesn't skimp its toilet, for we often see it giving itself a brisk and thorough cleaning of head, wings and legs. Surely it deserves a good mark for cleanliness! On the other hand, some of its habits are bad enough to make it nothing short of dangerous. So we won't sing its praises before learning more about its nature. Orderly persons that we are, we shall first try to put the fly in its proper place in the animal kingdom.

Where the fly belongs, and what distinguishes it from man

Naturalists are inquisitive. Not content with observing the outside of an animal, they always want to know what it looks like inside. For centuries they have been cutting up all kinds of animals and studying them from every angle. The knowledge they have gleaned fills volumes, but we shall leave those to the scientist and pick out only a few essentials from their store.

If we dissect a dead dog, a crow, or a lizard, a newt or a carp, we always find bones inside; they provide a firm support for the body and give it its shape. The spinal column is the axis of the skeleton, and from it spring the ribs to form the thorax. It carries the head in front and the bones of the limbs are connected with it by means of the shoulder and hip girdles. In spite of their many specific differences, the bones of a dog, an eagle or a carp all have the same basic structure and can easily be inferred from each other. Other physical characteristics also are unmistakably related; order-loving zoologists have therefore found it useful to place all mammals (including man), birds, reptiles, amphibians and fishes in one category or phylum and to call them vertebrates, after their most striking characteristic.

To get dry facts over and done with, we may add that, on the same principle of grouping together creatures that are similar, six other phyla of animals have been established: firstly, the protozoa (unicellular organisms), to which the most primitive animal forms belong. Some of these are too small to be seen by the naked eye, so that we can only appreciate their beauty when we look at them through a microscope; secondly, the hydrozoa with the coral polyps and the jelly-fish; then come the worms and the molluscs (including the snail, the shell-fish and the octopus), i.e. forms which are more familiar. The echinoderms, which include the sea-urchin and the starfish, are probably not unknown to most of us. The arthropods with all the crabs, the millipedes, the spiders and the insects form the largest and most varied phylum. And it is to this that the house-fly belongs.

Man has given the vertebrates the first place in this system, regarding himself as the lord and king of creation, but in actual fact it is not at all certain that the insects are not better developed. Today throughout the globe about 70,000 different species of vertebrates are known, but there are over a million different species of insects. Of all the kinds of animals of which we have any knowledge, three-quarters are insects. Nature has undoubtedly given them preferential treatment and has blessed them with unparalleled fecundity. For what are the masses of people that crowd our cities or even the uncountable shoals of herring compared with the insects swarming in one single wood? There, wood-ants build whole ranges of hills, each mound being a home for thousands of insects. Everything, from the tree-tops humming with industry to the moss-covered soil under foot, buzzes with the ceaseless activity of myriads of living creatures. The observant eye sees them and traces their every step, though most people are not alert enough to notice them.

Yet man loses no time about sitting up and taking notice once insects poach on his preserves. Then the lord of creation brings out all his big guns, though he does not always win the battle. When the nun, or night-moth, and other butterflies multiply too much for his convenience, he attacks them from the air and sprays insecticides on infested forests. He sends whole armies out to halt the advance of the Colorado beetle, even destroying his own crops in order to stamp out this pest. Though he spares neither money nor effort, he has not yet managed to rid the earth of troublesome insects: he must be content with keeping them within their proper bounds. And he does not always succeed in doing even that. In wide areas of Brazil, for instance, the best-laid schemes of planters have been wrecked only because of the existence there of leaf-cutter or parasol ants. They strip trees and shrubs bare with their sharp jaws, especially those with young, tender leaves, and do the job thoroughly. They carry their booty to their nests where they prepare a compost of the foliage for growing fungi, their main diet.

Now at last an effective way of combating them has been found—methylbromide. But no means has as yet been discovered of controlling the swarms of gnats and mosquitoes which render the vast tundras of Northern Asia uninhabitable in summer for civilized man. Nor can he do anything in the tropics about the voracious appetite of the termites which, invisible from the outside, hollow out beams and wooden supports of buildings until they finally collapse. So far the tiny insects have often proved to be the stronger opponents.

Although in those cases man is vanquished solely by force of numbers, the structure of the individual insect's body gives it an added advantage. In many respects it is equal or even superior to the human body; just that in their case Nature's method of solving problems of function differ from those she employs in vertebrates.

Insects have no vertebral column—indeed no bones at all. Instead they have an outer skin which gives them a firm frame. In it they are encased as completely as the medieval knight was in his coat-of-mail. But the insect's armour is made not of metal, but of chitin and protein, a superior material. It is hard, as you can feel if you touch a beetle, and yet so light that it scarcely hampers its wearer in flight.

Of the vertebrates, only the birds and the bats have mastered the secret of flying, and in acquiring this art many adaptations and radical modifications were necessary. To insects, on the other hand, flying came naturally, as it were. They beat their wings often at a tremendous speed. A house-fly can do this 200 times in a single second. We are lost in admiration of the dexterity of the violinist's fingers when he enchants us by playing trilled notes, but he actually touches the string only seven or eight times a second. It is also because the fly is so quick that it can so easily evade every attempt to catch or swat it. Has it then greater presence of mind than we? Perhaps it has merely a different sense of time, so that for a fly a second of time, in which it can beat its wings unhurriedly 200 times, is ample for a cruise through the air or long enough to make a leisurely escape from imminent danger.

If an insect were able to make comparative studies, it could only smile with pity at our breathing apparatus. We take air into our lungs through our two nostrils; the oxygen in the air is necessary for life in every part of our bodies. Not a muscle, not a single gland-cell, not the tiniest corner of our brain could live and work without oxygen. That is why the heart must pump constantly and drive the blood through the arteries. It supplies all the parts of the body with oxygen from the lungs with the help of no fewer than 25 billion red blood corpuscles. An insect has many "nostrils". They are located all along both sides of its body. They lead into tubes which ramify into a fine network of tiny vessels filled with air. These pass through all the organs and provide them with a direct supply of the oxygen they require. Could anything be simpler? So the heart has little to do: it is a thin tube which contracts without any great hurry, since its whole work consists in keeping juices and nourishment circulating throughout the body. The fly has no arteries such as we have, and therefore no arteriosclerosis either and no disturbances of the circulatory system.

And the amazing miracle of the insect's eye! In the case of the fly, the eyes take up practically the whole head; in other insects they are considerably smaller; but they are always composed of a great number of single eyes. Like minute telescopes, these eyes are packed closely together and can look in every direction at the same time. They register tiny sections of the field of vision, which are composed to form the complete image just as stones fit into a mosaic. Compared with our eye, where the image is formed on the retina, it is a different, but not a worse, way of seeing the world. In other respects these eyes are far superior to ours: their structural arrangement of light-sensory cells enables them, for instance, to recognize the plane of polarized light. The vibrations of the light rays coming from a blue sky are plane-polarized and occupy a certain position in relation to the sun. Our eyes are unable to discern the pattern of polarized light in a blue sky, but flies, bees, spiders and other arthropods can see it and are thus able, even if the sun is hidden by cloud, to infer its position from the smallest patch of blue sky. Since they are using the sun as a compass, this ability to respond to polarized light is of the utmost importance to them.

As far as smell and taste are concerned, many insects are far better off than we are. Their fine sense of smell has nothing to do with their many "nostrils", for their organs of smell are quite independent of their breathing apparatus, being situated in the antennae. How acute the fly's sense of smell is may be seen from the swarms that gather in a trice on decaying animal or vegetable matter, or on any freshly deposited excrement. These happen to be tit-bits for the fly. Their sense of taste is remarkable not only for its keenness but still more for the location of its organs. Many insects taste not only with the mouth-parts but also with the tip of their feet. A house-fly running round our breakfast table notices at once if it is treading on a drop of marmalade—a most convenient arrangement for creatures who are accustomed to find their food on the ground.

We have discussed only a few of the fly's organs. There is no need to do more. I merely wanted to show that insects are different from us in many things, and in many ways nearer perfection. In one respect, however, we are far superior, namely, in the development of our brain. Here they are on a much lower level. Their actions are mostly prompted by in-born instinct and not by reason, or reflection. This is another distinctive mark of this phylum of animals. Our relations with vertebrates can to a certain extent be more than merely physical. Our dog looks into our eyes trustfully, and we can make friends with a bird whose company we have enjoyed for some time; even so primitive a vertebrate as a salamander learns to know us and will come expectantly to the hand that offers it food. But, no matter how long we spend with a house-fly, we never make friends with it.

How to recognize a fly

Not all flies look alike. You may not have noticed that they differ in form and colour, and that they may even have different faces. But everyone will have noticed that there are big flies and small ones. I hope nobody thinks that the small flies are young ones. Actually, things are much the same with flies as with butterflies, where the larvae that emerge from the eggs have nothing in common with the adult insects: in the case of butterflies the larvae are called caterpillars; in the case of flies, maggots. A maggot grows into a pupa, out of which after a longish rest the winged insect appears as big then as it will ever be. So the big, fat bluebottles often found in the company of house-flies are not old, well-nourished specimens, but members of another species, just as ducks and geese are different species of birds.

We have all heard of people who make a life-long hobby of collecting beetles or butterflies. There are also people who collect flies. Most of us might not be attracted by the idea of collecting house-flies and fat bluebottles all our life. Yet more than 85,000 different species of flies have been described up to date. It can actually be a pleasure, indeed a passion, for lovers of Nature to stalk and observe flies, to collect and classify them. The variation in their habits and their shapes is astounding, though the observer will sometimes be unable to see them without the aid of a magnifying glass. There are also giants among them, big hairy creatures, more like bumble-bees; others have black and yellow markings that remind us of wasps; others again—the gnats—have an elongated abdomen, long, narrow wings and still longer legs. If you catch one of this species by the legs, you will find yourself left with legs between your fingers while their owners escape. The same thing happens when a bird snaps at them: they quickly amputate the leg that has been trapped—better life with five legs than death in the dark inside of a bird. But there are more varieties of flies than I can describe. However much they differ in appearance, all flies have one feature in common: insects as a rule have four wings. Every child who has drawn a butterfly knows the shape of its broad fore- and hind-wings. In bees and wasps the division between these is not so distinct, and you have to look carefully to see that they actually have four wings. When a may-bug settles, it tucks its fragile hind-wings under its heavy fore-wings—but four wings there are always. It is only the flies that make do with two wings, and that is why this order of insects is called "two-winged" (*Diptera*), a name given to it as long as 2000 years ago by Aristotle, the Greek philosopher and scientist.

To be quite exact, flies really do possess four wings just like the other insects, but the hind pair have degenerated: they can no longer aid in flying and are called balancers or halteres, serving now only as the site of sense organs.

Life history

Let us return to the house-fly. We know how it flies round and round lamps, we watch it climbing with the greatest of ease up the smooth surface of the window with the help of little sticky pads at the end of its legs, and we often find it enjoying a hearty meal at our breakfast table

Eggs, larva and pupa case of the bluebottle (*Calliphora erythrocephala*), a close relative of the house-fly.

without so much as a by-your-leave. But where was it born? Where does the mother-fly retire to when she wants to lay her eggs? We have grown so fond of her that I am ashamed to reveal her secret: she prefers to make her "nest" on pig-manure! Where there is none, on horse-manure or on any manure-heap in the open. In bad or cold weather, on manure in a warm stable or cowshed. And if that is not at hand, on any decaying matter that is equally unsavoury. Since it is not customary to keep manure or other decaying matter in our homes, we cannot observe the process of reproduction indoors, except for the brief union between males and females that takes place in mid-flight.

After about one day, or half a day if it is warm, the whitish maggots emerge from the eggs and fall on the decaying matter their mother has so kindly provided. They thrive on it and after about six days growth is complete. They have put on about 800 times their weight at birth. Just imagine a baby of 6-7 pounds at birth swelling in less than a week into a monster weighing about 4800 pounds! Here again, insects put man completely in the shade.

You cannot see the maggots growing. They stay under the surface of the dunghill—or wherever the mother has laid her eggs. If they are uncovered they wriggle out of sight very quickly—and wisely. For not only are they safe there from birds—early and late—but they need warmth and moisture, and would shrivel up in no time if they were exposed to the air.

When the maggot is fully grown, its outer skin hardens into a long, round, brown case, in which the pupa is hidden. It seems now as if life were extinct. But mysterious forces are at work under the hard case, transforming the flabby maggot into a winged insect. This process takes about a week, after which the fly bursts from the shell of the pupa to emerge into the light of day.

In their winged state, many insects live for only a few days or hours. Many at this final stage are not even equipped by Nature with anything in the way of a mouth, and are unable to eat. There is little sense in taking time to eat when life in any case is a matter of hours only, purposeless once the eggs are laid, a business in which little time is lost. The house-fly is not so short-lived. It begins to lay eggs about three days after abandoning the pupa case, and can still produce progeny two months later. Of course it must be well fed; we can see for ourselves any day that the fly has no use for fasting. It sips now fruit juice, now sweet dregs left at the bottom of a teacup, or it alights on a lump of sugar, which it taps with its proboscis and moistens with saliva so that the sugar dissolved in it can be sucked up; at other times it enjoys tit-bits that we would not like and that certainly would not like us.

A house-fly can lay about 100 eggs in one batch, about 1000 in the course of its life. If all the maggots hatched into flies and reproduced at the same rate, a single pair would produce 500,000 flies in the second generation, 250 million in the third, and in the fourth 125,000 million, i.e. more than six times the human population of the globe. If we remember how quickly one generation succeeds another, we can imagine that the descendants from one pair of flies would soon blacken the sky; we should be wading in flies and be suffocated in flies. This does not happen because most of them die at the larval stage, partly as a prey to countless foes, partly as the result of bad weather and other misfortunes. Once we realize how enormously they could increase under favourable conditions, we can no longer be surprised at the swarms of flies in or near stables and pig-sties with their perfect breeding places, or in southern countries with their favourable environment of warmth and dirt.

Where do house-flies spend the winter?

Autumn is a hard time for our house-flies. Cold days do not suit them at all. Still worse is a plague that works great havoc among them in late summer and autumn, when dead flies with twisted legs can often be seen on windows or walls, stuck fast to them by a filmy web of fungus threads. They are the victims of "fly-mould".

They have been attacked by a mould or fungus that starts growing inside their bodies, almost unnoticed at first. It swells till the victim shrivels up and dies. Then the fungus grows out of the "corpse" and scatters its spores, which will eventually destroy other flies.

A victim of fly-mould.

Yet just as the worst of plagues has never swept all men from the earth, not all flies are exterminated in autumn by this disease. The survivors have to see that their families get through the winter. Animals have different ways of getting over the cold weather. Many birds escape it by flying south, others put themselves on short rations and get through as best they can; the cross-bill alone is wise enough to make the seeds of conifers its main diet, so that it hatches its eggs when these are abundant, and can rear its young even in the iciest winter weather. For all kinds of deer winter is a weary time of fasting; the hamster feeds on what it has hoarded during the summer. In the insect world, the bees follow the same plan and get through the winter fairly well, if man does not take away too much of the honey they have harvested. Dormice, lizards and frogs preserve their lives by a long, deep winter-sleep: all the metabolic processes in their bodies slow down to a minimum, the fat they have stored in their bodies supplying all the food they need.

Very many insects live through the winter in sheltered places in the pupal stage, this being anyhow a time of rest. This was what the house-fly was thought to do. But though many species were seen to hatch from the great number of fly pupae collected in the open air during winter, the house-fly was not among them. House-flies seem to feel the cold very much and are evidently unable to survive the period of ice and snow in the open air, at least in countries with a severe climate. They live up to their name and are more attracted to dwellings and cowsheds in winter than in summer. Where there is manure, they can breed even in winter, though not so quickly as in the warm days of summer.

These little housemates of ours, then, belong to the few species of insects that do not dodge winter by hibernating. In towns, during the winter, their chances of breeding are few. Even in the country they have a hard struggle against disease and bad weather. How is it then that they appear again in full force and so quickly soon after the arrival of spring? The reason probably is that they are not really stay-at-homes. If they feel the urge to travel, they fly considerable distances. So when the weather is favourable they are soon dispersed from their breeding centres. Two American naturalists took the trouble to mark a quarter of a million flies with paint. Traps had been set over a wide area at varying distances from the place where the swarm of coloured flies was released and a great many of them were caught. Thousands had flown about one kilometre from the starting point, and some were caught after having flown up to twenty times as far. Such enterprising aeronauts have no difficulty in quickly spreading from a country area over a whole town, as has actually been proved.

How house-flies can be dangerous

We find house-flies a nuisance, particularly when they appear in swarms. But are they dangerous?

They leave tiny black specks wherever they settle for any time—signs of their good digestion. But they leave other traces, too; less obvious perhaps, but just as easy to detect: these are caused by the fly's habit of regurgitating tiny drops of food it has already swallowed. Their way of leaving droppings from both ends on whatever takes their fancy—sugar, bread, sausage, cake—is not exactly appetizing. Nausea is often the reaction of a sound instinct, as it is in this case. For the fly's dirty habits can be really dangerous to us.

We have seen that flies are not particular about what they eat. Their bill of fare includes cow droppings, human excrement (if available), the milk in our glass, or our sausage. Suppose, in the interest of clarifying our ideas, we forget the decrees of good manners and delicacy, and have a look at our own excrement through a strong microscope; if we look closely we shall see myriads of tiny living creatures in the now shapeless waste matter; these are the lowest form of vegetable life, the bacteria or bacilli. They live their lives hidden in our intestines and thrive on our meals, all unseen. They multiply so profusely that billions are evacuated with every stool. They are so tiny that it would take about five thousand of them laid end to end to make a daisy-chain long enough to go round a fly's head. Slender as the fly's proboscis is, the bacilli are much thinner still, so that they are easily sucked up and later ejected on to our food in the way we have described. So, blissfully ignorant, we consume the bacteria flies have already absorbed from the excreta of others. And that is usually harmless, though not always.

As a rule, the bacteria regularly found in the human intestine do no damage, but they may include dangerous germs. Typhoid fever, for instance, is caused by a certain kind of bacillus which multiplies enormously in a sick person, masses of them often being found in his stools. They have such a power of resistance that they cannot be digested by a fly and emerge from its anus as lively as ever. The same applies to tubercle bacilli and similar scallywags.

So we see how the house-fly may spread a fatal infection. The danger is all the greater because the fly's legs and mouth can also come into direct contact with filth. Naturally it won't have much opportunity to do so where cleanliness is the rule and where modern sanitation takes care of what flies hanker after. But if we think of habits in the country, of poverty and war, we shall understand the verdict of the doctors, which considered the fly-plague the most important cause of the great losses by the American forces in the Spanish-American War of 1898. During that campaign typhoid fever killed about ten times as many soldiers as Spanish bullets did, and flies were the chief carrier.

All this is ancient history, and things have greatly improved in the meantime, but the danger still exists even today, though to a lesser degree, and healthy people can become infected by flies with diseases like typhoid, dysentery, etc.

How flies help doctors

Fault-finding will now be followed by praise. For flies can be useful, though, to be accurate, this is less true of our house-fly than of its near relations—the fat bluebottle or the black-and-silver flesh-fly. They prefer to breed on decaying animals, bad meat, etc. The wriggling maggots the housewife is horrified to find under game that has lain too long in the larder are generally the larvae of bluebottles or flesh-flies.

Many insects refuse to touch anything except the food their parents and ancestors have lived on for centuries. There are butterfly caterpillars, for instance, which thrive only on one distinctive fodder-plant and would rather starve to death than eat the leaves of other plants, however closely related in species they may be. Flies are not so particular. If there is no decaying meat at hand, they have no objection to over-ripe cheese, or a festering sore. As long ago as Napoleon's day, army doctors had noticed that a wound swarming with maggots often healed amazingly well and quickly. The reason seemed to be that the maggots eat inflamed, morbid flesh and so cleanse the wound. Furthermore, their droppings stimulate the surface of the wound and so help the tissue to grow and the wound to close.

As a result of these observations American doctors had the courage deliberately to introduce maggots into wounds that were not healing well, above all in the case of obstinate inflammation of the bone-marrow. The poor maggots, it is true, had to put up with all manner of baths and cleansing processes to which they were not accustomed by Nature. Carried out in this way, the method has yielded good results. Nowadays better and more reliable methods are available, so we can dispense with the fly's medical services.

Biting flies

Who has not discovered that there are house-flies which bite? These, however, are not bad-tempered members of the house-fly family but a different species, though very similar in size, shape and colour. The scientific name of the former is *musca domestica*, i.e. the house-fly, while zoologists have given the latter the imposing name of *stomoxys calcitrans*. Stomoxys means "sharp mouth" and that indicates the characteristic difference between the two species. Instead of the house-fly's suction proboscis with a harmless lobe at the end (see figure on p. 9) for dropping liquid, the stinging or gad-fly may easily be recognized by its protruding stylet. Another difference is that when they squat, their wings are farther apart. They are just as annoyingly persistent as the house-fly. We may flip them off our legs ten times and back they will come to bite us another ten times. Not that they delight in teasing us, but just because they want to feed on blood as Nature has decreed.

It is a good thing for us that the gad-fly is more attracted to cattle than to human beings. They sometimes distress cows so much that their supply of milk suffers. Gad-flies also like to settle on horses and other domestic animals, and sometimes, quite harmlessly, on juicy fruits. In autumn their love of warmth drives them indoors and we become more

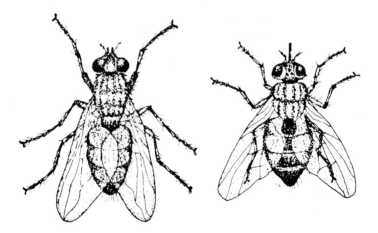

House-fly (*left*). Gad-fly (*right*). The gad-fly's protruding stylet and the different posture of its wings make it easy to distinguish between the two species. (Magnified about 3 times.)

aware of their presence. Hence the myth that house-flies begin to bite in autumn.

Their habits are similar to those of the house-fly, and they develop in the same way. Having saved the house-fly's honour by showing that the two species are not identical, we shall take leave of its bad-tempered counterpart.

Protection from the house-fly pest

House-flies can become a pest in houses situated near cow-sheds, dunghills and similar places where flies like to breed. We do not intend to discuss here ways and means of reducing their numbers by taking hygienic measures in cow-sheds or by special methods of treating dunghills. We accept their existence and are only interested in knowing how to rid ourselves of flies in our homes.

In the past, fly paper used to be the favoured remedy indoors. Today we combat the house-fly with formulations based on dichlorvos or lindane and pyrethrum (see footnote on p. 32) applied by aerosol dispenser or in the form of a dusting powder. Chemists and hardware shops also sell impregnated plastic strips, known as Vapona Pest Strips, which may be hung up where flies are particularly troublesome. Details of approved insecticides and recommended control measures against not only flies, but all the other domestic pests discussed in this book, will be found in the Advisory Leaflets of the Ministry of Agriculture, Fisheries and Food*. However, here, as elsewhere, prevention is better than cure. The best thing is not to let the flies into the house at all, then there will be no need to devise means of combating them. Screens can be fixed to windows and doorways, though of course they reduce the supply of light and air. And flies can be kept out if care is taken to shut the windows before the sun comes, for they enter the house only through windows on which the sun shines. The saying that a closed mouth catches no flies applies to our houses too. So if you must let the sun in, you will just have to put up with the flies.

---

* Single copies are obtainable free of charge from Ministry of Agriculture, Fisheries and Food (Publications), Tolcarne Drive, Pinner, Middlesex HA5 2DT.

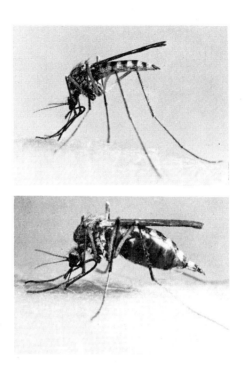

Gnat. Starting to bite (*top*). Replete at the end of the bite
(*bottom*). The proboscis, for biting and sucking, lies in a sheath
which is open at the front and which bends backward in a loop
when the proboscis is in action. The lower end of the sheath
acts as guide and support while the skin is being pierced.

Gnats

Gnats, the common mosquitoes of America, are "flies", too. It is true
that their tapering, slender body and their long, fine legs make them
look different from the stout bluebottles. But we must not let ourselves
be misled by mere looks. Gnats have only two wings and therefore they
are flies. As with all members of this group, the hind-wings are

24

represented by small balancers. When one is in the right mood, solitary specimens of the house-fly may not be unpleasant. But gnats— sometimes called midges—can never be pleasant. They have a treacherous—and often silent—mode of attack and we don't feel them piercing our skin with their fine proboscis, but their bites itch all the more intensely.

Why gnat bites itch

Many people classify animals as either useful or harmful. Actually they are surprised that there is such a thing as a harmful animal: they simply cannot get rid of the idea that man walks the earth as the centre of creation and that everything else is there merely to serve him.

Anyone who looks round with open eyes will form a very different picture. He will notice that the humblest of living creatures are just as well equipped for the hard struggle for existence as the arrogant human race. We have already seen that the insect's breathing organs compare not unfavourably with our own; in gnats the organs of flight reach a high level of perfection, and every mechanic must admit that their proboscis is a masterpiece of ingenuity as regards both structure and mechanism. Why has Nature decreed that their bites should itch? Would it not be better for them if their contact with us were painless? We should not then have any occasion to swat them when we catch them biting us. There is plenty of evidence, however, to show that the irritation we feel is only the necessary consequence of an arrangement that is very convenient for the gnat.

The sight of a delicious dish makes our mouth water, which is only a short way of saying that the very sight of food stimulates our salivary glands to produce the secretion that helps us to swallow and digest it. The gnat, too, has salivary glands, and its mouth waters when it settles to have a meal off us, though here the purpose is different: after it has pierced the skin, it deposits through the proboscis a tiny drop of liquid, which acts as a poison. It irritates the surrounding tissues and quickly produces a local inflammation. This is connected with an expansion of the blood vessels, which in turn leads to an increased flow of blood, as the redness round the puncture shows. We feel the effect of the poison as pain, and that may be fatal for the gnat. And yet this droplet, so inconvenient to us, is essential to the gnat, since it alone makes it possible for the hair-like proboscis to get at the food. In addition, the gnat's saliva has the extraordinary property of preventing the blood from congealing, so that the narrow passage of the proboscis cannot be blocked by any clot.

It is lucky for gnats that cattle are not so sensitive as we are. In spite of the irritation caused by their bites, they are often allowed to finish their meal in peace.

General remarks on blood-sucking

In a certain sense gnats are specialists as far as food is concerned. We never see them settling like house-flies on sugar or bread, on meat or unsavoury waste matter. They want to feed on blood, and it must be that of warm-blooded animals. Newts or lizards are not good enough for them, but they are not particular whether they get their nourishment from a human being, or a cow, or a bird. Man is by no means their only victim. When considering their lust for blood we must make one important reservation: it is only the female gnats that suck blood. Nor are they a reprehensible exception in this respect, for there are other similar cases. Blood-sucking gad-flies, for instance, which often spoil the pleasure of bathing, and other big, fat horse-flies, sometimes a plague near cattle pastures, are always females. The males disport themselves on flowers and sip honey.

Is this because the females have a particularly malicious temper? Not really. There is good reason for this difference in the activities of the sexes. The female needs her meal of blood to bring her eggs to maturity.

How a pest on land comes originally from water

Gnats constitute a pest only near accumulations of water, and the reason is not far to seek: they must have water if they are to reproduce. The females lay their eggs on the surface of water (see figure on p. 27); many species lay also on damp ground, whence the eggs are washed into puddles by rain. When the larvae emerge, they dive down into the water and stay there during the entire period of development. Under favourable conditions this takes only about a week, but considerably

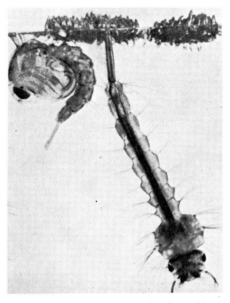

The eggs of the gnat, or common mosquito, float all in a clump
on the water like a toy boat. The larva (*right*) and the pupa (*left*)
live in the water, but breathe air on the surface through tubes.
(Magnified about 7 times.)

longer if the weather is cool or food is scarce. In contrast to their
mother, the larvae are harmless vegetarians and make do with some
decaying vegetable matter; many species prefer animal food, and the
myriads of tiny creatures living in the water provide a varied bill of fare.

One end of their bodies has access to the air, from which they have
come, for their respiratory organs must be supplied with air under
water, too. The larvae of our common gnat breathe in the air they
require through a fine tube, by which they are usually suspended from
the surface (see figure). From here they wriggle down below on
occasional voyages of exploration.

The pupae of the gnat are not the barrel-shaped hard cases
characteristic of house-flies. On the contrary, they are lively little devils.
While the larva is supplied with oxygen from the rear, the pupa has two

short breathing-tubes perched like horns on its head end (see figure on p. 27). After two or three days in the pupal stage, the winged insect emerges. It floats about on the raft-like empty pupa case until its wings are dry and strong enough to carry it ashore.

The swarms of dancing midges or gnats which sometimes rise in the air like smoke consist exclusively of males. The females only dart in to snatch a mate and to elope with him for the brief nuptial flight.

Brackish water, ponds and pools, even small puddles and water-butts are favourite breeding-places. Important as the water-barrel is for gardening, it is often a source of torment for those who frequent the garden. Only the cold of autumn checks the reproductive activity in many unheeded pools, which brings forth generation after generation of gnats to annoy us. When the weather gets colder, they seek protection indoors, above all in the cellars of houses, where thousands can be seen hibernating on ceilings and walls. So it is not till this season of the year, when mercifully they are not bloodthirsty, that they actually become our housemates.

The gnat or mosquito pest is worst in the tundra and watery plains of Siberia, Lapland and Northern Canada, where these insects make it practically impossible for man to settle, and in many countries of South America and Southern Asia: the notorious mosquitoes of these regions are very closely related to our gnats. It is easy to understand their abundance in the tropics, since they need water and love warmth. But it is not so clear why such swarms of them should be found in Arctic regions. In Lapland snow lies on the ground for eight months of the year. Why should these little pests feel so comfortable in a country where they will search in vain for cellars to protect them from the severe winter, where there is little rain during the short summer and where for miles and miles there are neither human beings nor cattle to supply their food requirements?

Much attention has been paid to this problem in recent years, particularly in Lapland. And the riddle has been solved. These species of gnats or mosquitoes do not survive the winter. It is only the eggs they have laid in the moist soil that survive. In spring these get into the numerous pools formed by melting snow. Although the soil consists of porous peat and is not washed by tropical rains, these pools remain for an astonishingly long time. The reason becomes apparent if a stick is pushed through the loose soil. It meets with resistance barely half a metre down. At that depth the ground is still frozen, which prevents the water from seeping away. But the pools on the surface of this ice-bound soil become amazingly warm, since in those latitudes they are exposed to the sun's rays day and night. Such shallow pools take weeks to dry up. Meanwhile the gnats can breed in abundance. Though there may be very few human beings and reindeer for them to attack when they swarm up into the air, there are millions of lemmings and voles, which serve their purpose equally well, probably the last thing that the traveller in Lapland would think of when he is racking his brain to find an explanation for the many gnats.

Mosquitoes as fever-carriers

Whoever travels by train south of Rome to Naples will pass through the Pontine Marshes. What a few years ago was a malaria-infested country, inhabited—as in Roman times—by a few needy shepherds, is now a prosperous province. Thanks to extensive drainage the marshes have been dried and arable land has replaced poor pastures.

It was not actually the marshes that kept this region from being cultivated for long centuries. There would have been room for farms between the swamps. All who settled there, however, were unfailingly attacked by a severe fever, attributed formerly to bad air from the marshes. The real connexion is different and interesting enough to be considered more closely.

The disease in question is known as malaria or intermittent fever. It is not of course confined to the Pontine Marshes; even today, it occurs in other parts of Southern Europe, in Russia and Holland and occasionally in Central Europe, while it is one of the worst plagues in tropical areas in all continents. It is called intermittent fever because as a rule violent attacks alternate regularly with fever-free days. In many cases this fever is fatal, and in many others its ill effects are lasting. Scientists have discovered that malaria is caused by microscopically small unicellular animals of very simple structure, which live in the blood of the sick person. Simplicity of structure is not always connected with a simple way of life. The little parasites make very special demands on life and if everything does not happen in the way they are used to, they just perish. To begin with, they require as their habitat the red corpuscles in human blood. These are minute cells from the tremendous numbers of which the red colour of our blood is derived. They are quite invisible to the naked eye, but big enough for the still smaller parasites to grow and multiply in. Every time a parasite has eaten its way through a corpuscle, it attacks another, and since development, once started, is fairly regular in the warmth of the blood, all the parasites change quarters at practically the same time. This is when the fever becomes violent. It is the body's reaction to the poisons released from the decaying blood cells as soon as they are deserted by the parasites. When the latter have found new quarters in other red corpuscles, the patient enjoys fair health until the next change of quarters. They multiply so profusely that they can be detected in the tiniest drop of blood.

There are two sides to the life of such a parasite. The better the unbidden guest thrives, the more dangerous he is to his host, but if he kills his host, he deprives himself of his daily bread. From the parasite's point of view, therefore, it is expedient for some of them to emigrate to another human body in good time. For this passage they make use of a mosquito as a carrier. When a mosquito sucks blood from a sick person, it pumps up the parasites along with the blood. They settle down comfortably for some time in the wall of the mosquito's stomach and multiply at its expense. Then, guided by some invisible force, they slip into the mosquito's salivary glands. So when the mosquito later bites a healthy person, it injects the parasite with its saliva into his blood and he becomes ill. This is the only way of catching malaria and it can be spread by only one genus of gnat (*Anopheles*, the fever-gnat or malaria mosquito).

Nobody knows why none of the other species of this insect either in our temperate zone or in the tropics is good enough to carry the malaria parasite.

Although the malaria mosquito is fairly widespread in Central Europe, it hardly ever poses a serious threat. To do so, other conditions must be present, e.g. a warm climate to enable the parasites to develop rapidly, and malaria carriers among the population, for if the mosquito has no opportunity to become infected with the parasites, it cannot transmit them and its bite will be harmless.

The Italian Government did a fine bit of work when it drained the Pontine Marshes and destroyed the breeding-places of the mosquitoes, thus restoring the country to health. But the scholars who, in the seclusion of study and laboratory, revealed the chain of cause and effect that first made it possible to combat the disease did a still finer job.

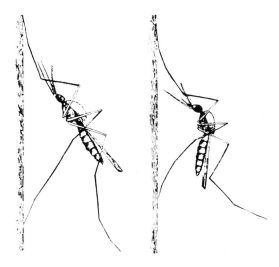

The different posture when it settles distinguishes the malaria mosquito (*left*) most clearly from the gnat or common mosquito (*right*).

Efforts must be made to exterminate the mosquito; where there are no carriers, there will be no malaria. There are many ways of reaching or approaching this goal. In the case of the Pontine Marshes drainage made it impossible for the mosquitoes to breed. Another method is to let the mosquito's natural foes do man's work for him. Fishes, water-beetles or the larvae of the dragon-fly, all voracious eaters of the mosquito's young, have been introduced into potential breeding-places of the insect. In our latitudes the greedy stickleback and certain species of small white fish have proved their worth, whereas in warmer climes toothed carps, small fish which have been popular with aquarists ever since they were first imported from South America at the turn of the century, have been most successful. Their popularity is deserved for they are hardy and multiply rapidly, hence they are generally known as "million fish". The species is of some zoological interest because in the male the anal fin has become transformed into a copulatory organ and the female hatches its eggs within its abdomen and gives birth to live young. Aquarists are also familiar with the gambusias (*Gambusia affinis*) and the guppy (*Poecilia reticulata*), both of them keen exterminators of mosquito larvae. As such they have been introduced by man into the waters of all the tropical mosquito areas.

In the past, petroleum was often poured on the water. The resulting film on the surface blocked the insects' breathing tubes (see figure on p. 27), thereby causing them to suffocate. But this meant polluting the water and endangering aquatic life as a whole. Various synthetic substances have also been added to the water in an effort to poison the larvae, but not being specific, they are always liable to harm other living organisms as well. Hence the number of people advocating the use of fish to "police" the water is growing. Ultimately the money available and local conditions will determine which method is best in each individual case.

Without the threat of malaria being present, it will hardly be necessary to combat the mosquito on quite the same scale. Nevertheless, most people will prefer not to be pestered by them, or by their fat relative, the gad-fly, in the garden or on the beach. Protection against them is afforded by various repellents. Containing approved substances like dichlorvos, pyrethrum*, and others, these ointments or sprays retain their efficacy for several hours. For indoor use fly spray aerosol dispensers are recommended.

---

* Pyrethrum is a bush-like perennial belonging to the marguerite family, but a native of warm countries. The flowers, dried and finely ground, contain substances which are poisonous to insects and which are an essential ingredient of many insecticides marketed under different trade-names. They often also contain chemicals—synergists—which, while not being poisonous to the insects, increase the toxicity of pyrethrum, thus permitting a lower concentration to be used.

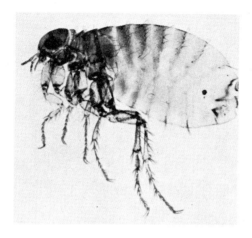

Microscopic picture of female human flea.

The Flea

The reader who has got thus far will by now know a little about zoology. He will have an idea of what insects are; he will know that he can recognize flies by the fact that they have two wings and so he will be able to distinguish them from the four-winged representatives of this class in the animal kingdom. He will now be keen enough to put a flea—if he can get hold of one—under his magnifying-glass and try to discover how many wings it has. He won't find any, for the flea has no wings. And so what? How are we to put it in its proper place?

Fleas are certainly insects. But what kind of insect? Experts are not at all certain. As a rule the best clue is provided by the wings and their veining, which varies considerably from group to group. Here the flea does not help us. As a matter of fact its very earliest ancestors did possess wings, as is proved by the tiny wing-buds on every flea in the pupa stage, which however recede as development progresses. It has learnt to jump so well that wings became superfluous. And now we have to guess where it comes from. Some think that it is descended from the

33

beetle, others from the *Hemiptera*, the order which numbers the blood-sucking bed-bug among its members. The theory most widely held is that it is descended from the fly. The many peculiarities of its structure, however, have led scientists to honour it by giving it an "order" of its own, just as the beetles, the flies, etc., each form a separate order of insects.

To sum up, then, the flea is probably a close cousin of the fly. But it is not a fly: it is a flea.

What a flea looks like, and what it can do

For most people a flea is probably just a black speck, which jumps away when they try to catch it. It takes a very strong magnifying glass to bring out details. Whoever has a microscope and a flea at hand should try to bring them together. What he will see is shown in the illustration on page 33. If we want to understand what we see, we must bear in mind that the flea family does not regard man as the central figure in its world. The many fleas on dogs, cats, mice and other mammals, in the feathers of innumerable birds outnumber by far the few that settle on human beings.

That is why its body is so made that it can pass unhindered through thick fur, or feathers. It is flattened from side to side and so has no difficulty in passing through the densest hair-forest, its keel-shaped forehead forcing its way through the undergrowth like the bows of a boat cleaving the waves. The proboscis (marked P in the figure on p. 39) slopes down and backwards; the antennae (A in the upper drawing) can lie back in grooves in the head. Its shape is not like that of other insects (compare the illustration on p. 9); there is no thin neck separating the head from the thorax and no slender waist between the thorax and the abdomen. Nothing is allowed to break the streamlining of its body—no bulge or notch to get entangled when the flea creeps through hair or feathers. The strong bristles slope backwards and serve the insect as a support when it moves about, while the strong claws on its feet ensure a good foothold. The hindmost pair of legs are particularly sturdy. These are the flea's jumping legs. They are vitally important to the flea not only for making its get-away, but also as a means of leaping onto a passing animal or human in search of its next meal. A flea can jump

more than 10 centimetres high and more than three times as far. Of
course that is not much. But translated into human terms, an adult
man wanting to compete with a flea would have to clear the high-jump
bar at about 100 metres and his long jump would have to measure
about 300 metres. Such an athlete would have no difficulty in vaulting
over Victoria Station in London. At one jump he could leap from
Westminster Bridge to the top of Big Ben.

The flea's jumping ability does not depend solely on muscular
strength. It derives from a tiny ligament consisting of protein—resilin—
which is built into the jumping mechanism and is more elastic than any
rubber band. When getting ready to jump, the flea tenses this ribbon
by muscular action, releasing it suddenly for take-off. This adds
enormously to the muscle power and explains the speed and magnitude
of the leap.

The flea's eyes are poorly developed and can certainly not tell a man
from a tree trunk. Perhaps to them moving shapes appear as shadows.
More important are the organs of smell, located on the antennae. Not
much is known about the flea's sensory experiences. We shall return to
this subject presently.

The life history of a flea

Fleas make indifferent mothers! While the house-fly at least takes
the trouble to lay her eggs in manure and the gnat finds a puddle for the
same purpose, so as to ensure the proper living conditions for their
broods, a flea simply lets her eggs drop. Whether or not they land on a
good place is left entirely to chance.

As a rule fleas breed best in the floors of houses. The maggots, which
are hatched from the eggs after about three days, are like white worms

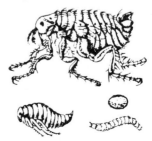

The eggs of the flea are relatively large. The egg
of a human flea (*bottom, right, upper sketch*) and
adult human flea shown here are on the same
scale (magnified about 10 times). Flea larva
(*bottom, left*), not yet fully developed. Flea pupa,
taken out of its cocoon (*bottom, right, lower
sketch*).

(see figure on p. 35) and can wriggle quickly in much the same way as caterpillars. They have a preference for dusty crevices and cracks in floors, or for carpets and rugs, and dusty corners in beds and other pieces of furniture. They are not interested in blood-letting. They feed on all kinds of waste, which they find in dust. After about a fortnight they spin a cocoon for themselves like, say, the silk-moth butterfly, and retire inside to pupate. After another week or two, the flea emerges fully fashioned. On an average it can live 3-4 months. While starving it remains inactive and can reach the age of 1-1½ years.

It may be a male or a female, the male being the slimmer and smaller of the two. Both are bloodthirsty and lie in wait to spring on a victim, usually from the ground. How can they recognize their prey in spite of their undeveloped eyes? Perhaps they notice a shadow, perhaps they feel the warmth of a near body, or the current of air caused by movement; the sense of smell also plays an important part; otherwise it would be difficult to understand why they favour many people, show less preference for others and avoid some completely, since there can be little difference in their shadows or body temperature.

Some 60 years ago I was in Naples with a friend on one of my visits to the Zoological Station there, where I have often worked. We had taken a room high up in the Vomero. The marvellous view over the blue Gulf to the lovely contours of Capri that greeted us when we woke was in itself a promising start to every day. The nights were not so good, for the place was alive with fleas. We soon hit on a way of getting a fair night's sleep. Before getting into bed we would parade up and down the room barefoot and in our nightshirts, to be immediately attacked by a hungry army. Then we would take our night-shirts off and hunt for fleas. My "bag" every night amounted to a mere four or five, whereas my friend always caught thirty or forty. They seemed to prefer him; he had evidently a better smell in the opinion of fleas. In spite of this, he suffered less than I did, for he was only annoyed by their creeping, while I got a big bump from every bite. So the skin of different individuals does not react to bites in the same way at all, and the same is true of bites of other insects.

The amount of saliva a flea injects into the wound it makes is incredibly small. It has been calculated at 0.00004 of a cubic millimetre. This means that it would take more than one and a half million fleas to produce enough poison to equal the quantity of liquid in an ordinary drop of water. We can imagine the virulence of the poison when we consider that one such drop would set some two million people scratching, provided we could ensure that they all received their proper dose. This we could not do, since unfortunately we lack an instrument as precise as the flea's sucking tube.

If this little pest is left to suck in peace, it takes its time. It can enjoy one and the same puncture for several hours. As a rule, of course, irritation makes the host interrupt the process and the flea has to continue its meal elsewhere.

The flea's love-concert

The female flea must find a mate before eggs can be laid. This may not be quite easy, either on the floor of a house, on a human body or on a dog's skin. The sense of smell will certainly help, but not when the couple are far apart. Fleas evidently have another means of making their desires known. At the roots of the hind legs there are rows of little spikes; with certain leg movements these spikes twitch the fine ridges on the abdomen opposite them, in the same way as the harpist's fingers pluck the strings of his instrument. We are familiar with the very similarly constructed organs used for chirping by crickets, grasshoppers and other insects. Their notes are quite audible to our ears, whereas in the case of the flea the whole musical instrument is so minute and the notes it makes so faint and probably so highly pitched that it takes the ear of a flea to hear them. Scientists have not yet found out where the flea's ears are located just as no one has ever heard its voice. For the biologist it is a stimulating and not at all incredible idea that ears capable of hearing it should be able to catch a many-voiced chorus from the thick pelt of an Alsatian, similar to the concert of crickets and grasshoppers we hear in meadows.

My driving test

At last the day had come when I was to have my driving test. Accompanied by my instructor I arrived in good time to pick up the police officer in charge of the ordeal. Armed with paper and pencil with which to note my mistakes, he settled down in the back seat—not exactly soothing for the candidate. Now we were ready to start. Nothing happened, and no wonder, since I had forgotten to use the ignition-key, which drew some comment from the rear. Then things went all right as I drove round several corners. All at once the officer asked: "Is it true, Professor, that fleas are dying out?" I hadn't expected such a question. But I knew more about fleas than about a car, and we talked at such length on the subject that there was no time for the officer to set me more difficult problems in the art of driving, which was really what he was there for.

It was a question that was arousing quite a lot of interest just then, filling columns in the daily press. It was suggested that a plague had destroyed the fleas. They had become so rare that a shop that supplied teaching material was said to pay several Reichsmarks for one flea. The firm, it is true, denied this emphatically, asserting that it could produce any number of fleas at any time. Yet when I asked for some for demonstration purposes a little later, they regretted they could not give me any.

There is no doubt that the flea plague has been greatly reduced in our part of the world in the last half-century. Some of the reasons are obvious. Modern vacuum cleaners make short work of the dust in corners and cracks (so necessary to the flea), the habit of wiping floors with wet cloths, which supplied the brood with the moisture it required, is gradually dying out, while central heating makes rooms still drier, which spells death for the larvae. And the polishes now popular for treating floors are poisonous for them. So growing cleanliness and hygiene in the home often destroy the larvae's chance of survival and lead to the decline of the flea population.

Whether these reasons are sufficient to account for the reduction in our population of fleas, or whether it has actually been decimated by some infectious disease, we cannot tell. At any rate such a disease cannot have spread very far, for travellers to the South or the East will not be slow to realize that the flea is certainly not dying out there.

About various species of fleas

Nobody is astonished that collecting butterflies can be a pleasure.

But that a rich man with a penchant for scientific research should have concentrated entirely on collecting fleas from all parts of the world at considerable cost to his pocket is not so easy to understand. Yet his interest in collecting fleas proved most valuable, as we shall see very soon.

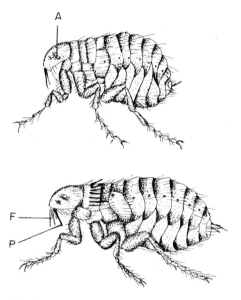

(*Above*) A human flea. (*Below*) A dog flea. A = antenna, F = mouth-feeler, P = proboscis for piercing and sucking. (Both are magnified 20 times.)

Just as there are many different kinds of butterflies or birds, there are also many kinds of fleas. Since they are so small, they can only be distinguished with the help of a microscope. As a result of extensive studies, in which the collection referred to above played an important part, about 1000 different species of fleas are known today, of which 150 are to be found in Europe. That they differ in appearance will leave most people cold, though more interest will be shown in their varying tastes. What has been said up to now applies mainly to the human flea.

Luckily for us, most species will have nothing to do with human blood, but live on certain birds and mammals. A flea from a swallow was starved for nine months and then put on a human being. It began at once to suck, but stopped again immediately; when it was examined, it was clear that the blood was so distasteful to the flea that it had not even got as far as its gullet. Birds are often very badly plagued by fleas, and their nests are breeding-places for the parasites.

The smallest mammal—the shrew—has the biggest flea. The flea is also found on moles, hence its name: "the big mole flea". It is more than half a centimetre long. If we compare this with the length of a shrew's body, the fleas that visit us would have to be as big as rats. Hedgehogs, too, are a happy hunting ground for fleas. Bats, rabbits, pigeons, hens and many other animals all have their own fleas.

Now it is not that a definite species of flea is invariably found on a definite species of mammal or bird. Many species like to vary their diet. The hen flea, for instance, was found on no less than 48 different kinds of birds. The human flea, for instance, also likes dogs and has been found on badgers, foxes and hedgehogs. Vice versa, the dog flea also preys on human beings. A spot check proved to what extent this is true: of 2000 fleas collected at random from all sorts of human beings, half were dog fleas. Not so often, but still not seldom do cat fleas, hen fleas and pigeon fleas desert their usual host, after which they are named, in order to suck human blood. That the rat flea does this may be fatal to us. Which brings me to the usefulness of a scientific collection of fleas.

The flea and the bubonic plague

If our interest in recognizing forms had not extended to this unpopular insect, if our delight in varying shapes had stopped short at this, the smallest order, our eye would never have been trained to distinguish between the many hundreds of flea species. Then perhaps the rat flea would have remained unknown and its disastrous role in spreading the bubonic plague would never have been discovered.

This disease, like typhoid fever, is caused by a particular kind of bacterium. They are far more malignant than the typhoid bacilli. If a man is attacked by the bubonic plague he has little chance of survival. In India it kills hundreds of thousands every year. It was already known that it could attack rodents as well as human beings, and that it was rampant among rats. But the casual connexion between the rat plague and the human plague was not detected till later, and the rat flea was found to be the most dangerous carrier. When it sucks the blood of diseased rats, it absorbs plague bacilli at the same time. These live in the flea's intestine and multiply there, sometimes for months on end. The flea can eject lively plague bacilli both in its saliva and in its excrement, thus spreading the infection. As long as the infection is confined to rats, we are not interested, but heavy casualties among rats as a result of the plague mean famine for fleas, and they must look round for another source of nourishment. Then the risk arises of their settling in considerable numbers on human beings. So a violent epidemic of plague in rats often heralds a similar outbreak among the human population.

The flea circus

Troupes of performing fleas used to be a familiar attraction at fairs and other festivities. Whether their antics are not exciting enough for modern spectators, or whether the declining flea population has produced a shortage of trainees, whatever the reason may be, such performances are seldom seen or heard of these days.

Actually such a show was never of the kind offered by other performing animals, say at Hagenbeck's or Sanger's circus. The real artiste in the flea circus is not the flea, but its trainer. He knows how to fix a harness of fine silver or copper wire so cleverly round the breast of his fleas that they cannot slip through. Then the flea is suspended from

A loop of fine silver wire is fixed round the performing flea's breast.

a chain, not of course the kind of chain that tethers the watch-dog, but one suited to the tiny captives, now fettered for life. The only thing the fleas must learn for their performance is that it no longer pays to jump.

After spending some days or weeks in the vain attempt to take off, they resign themselves to walking.

At this stage it is again the dexterous trainer who makes them display their extraordinary strength. He arranges races between Lilliputian teams harnessed to a gala coach of thin sheet brass or to a paper carriage; or he fixes a tiny sword under a foreleg and delights his young audience by staging miniature duels. To heighten the fun, the participants may be clad in coats-of-mail; others, dressed as ballet dancers, dance in a ring. As a grand finale, the showman astonishes his audience (and perhaps makes their flesh creep a little) by turning up his sleeves and rewarding his performers by letting them refresh themselves on his blood. It seems a pity that the flea circus is dying out.

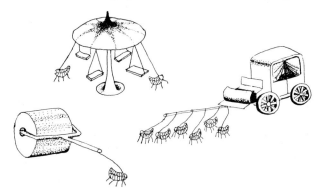

In a flea circus.

The amber flea

All the remarkable things we have learnt about fleas will not, I am afraid, raise them in the estimation of most people. Yet in one respect they have a right to look down on us. I am not thinking of their jumping feats, which outshine by far those of any human champions, nor of the efficacy of their poison, which might have called forth the envy of medieval potion-brewers, but of their age in the history of the earth. If fleas understood these things they would look down their noses at us as a contemptible rabble of parvenus.

Remains of animals and plants from bygone ages have often come down to us as fossils. No fossilized fleas have been found. It is of course quite credible that fleas should have got into muddy deposits and that when these solidified they should have left petrified impressions there. But who would attempt today to look for such a fossilized flea in the conglomeration of rocks?

And yet some decades ago a flea was actually discovered that had lived in the Eocene Period of the Tertiary Age, that is, about 60 million years ago. At that time it had, by some mischance or other, had the bad luck to stick to a clammy drop of pine-tree resin. It was immured in an air-tight prison that hardened, and is thus better preserved than an Egyptian mummy.

Amber, the present form of this antediluvian discharge of resin, is much sought after in the market today. Where the movement of the waves washes it out of old deposits—as at the bottom of the Baltic—it is eagerly collected on the shore. Zoologists keep a sharp look-out for amber, since all kinds of insects came to a sticky end in the ideal fly-paper provided by the yellow drop of resin; they have been preserved so well in it that the student today can look at them through his magnifying-glass and count the bristles on their legs or study all the details of the veining on their wings. And so the amber flea got into the hands of a zoologist. He found that it belonged to a genus that has practically the same form today. For long it was a unique specimen, but a second example of exactly the same kind has recently turned up. Perhaps this genus annoyed shrews in the forest primeval as it does today.

The beginnings of the human race can be traced back about one million years in the history of the earth. Yet 60 million years ago a mouse-flea was jumping about in the shape it has today. Is this not enough to inspire us with a little respect for the flea?

The Bed-bug

It is not exactly pleasant for those who set store by cleanliness and look askance at vermin to discover a flea in their immediate surroundings; but to find bugs in the house is nothing short of a catastrophe.

Why do we not find these two parasites equally repulsive? Is it because bugs are bigger? Or because we see them running away while a flea escapes from our sight at one jump? Or because bug-bites are more painful? Because they lust for our blood as soon as they can breathe, whereas fleas begin life by crawling unseen in the dust? Or is it because bugs have a nasty smell, or because they are more difficult to get rid of?

Why bugs should make us squirm—or, rather, should have made us squirm, for improved housing conditions have made them something of a rarity—will always be their secret. But their unpleasant qualities should not prevent us from paying them some attention.

A plea for justice

To avoid any misunderstanding, I should like to make it clear straight away that I have no desire to defend the bed-bug. I am only anxious that we should not condemn wholesale all the 40,000 species of bugs that have been recognized up till now. Many of them use their mouth parts in order to feed fairly harmlessly on plant juices as their close cousins, the plant-lice and the cicadas, do. Big green, brown or red and black striped bugs living on trees are a common and striking sight on the tops of big blossoms and on leaves. They are not shy and have no desire to hide; their unpleasant smell is a good protection against greedy enemies.

When picking raspberries, many of us may have come across the odd berry with a rather nauseating taste, the result of a recent visit by one of these bugs. Their protective substance, produced by a special gland, can penetrate on contact the protective armour of other insects and can even kill them. Man was so proud of his new contact poison DDT that he bestowed the Nobel Prize upon its discoverer, yet bugs have been using the same principle for millions of years.

Nor do all bugs smell. Many species do not offend sensitive nostrils in the least. Thousands of little bugs, often attractive in colour, may be found among the many insects that swarm peacefully and happily in a summer meadow. The biologist, interested as he is in all forms of life, would be sorry if they were not there. Many of them pursue other insects, lay them low by an injection of their poisonous saliva and then suck them dry.

A large group of bugs has adapted itself to an aquatic existence and remains therefore relatively little known. In America, South Africa and India there are some veritable giants which can grow to 11 centimetres in length, or longer than an adult's index finger. Some of the largest insects in existence today, they feed on salamanders, frogs and fishes. It is just as well that they are water creatures, for the thought of one of these giants attacking man to feast on his blood is hardly a pleasant one.

Very few venture to attack birds or mammals. It is a short step from highway robber to parasite and one that is easy to explain. The booty they select is too big to kill and consume, so the robber becomes a blood-sucking parasite. And it is these blood-suckers that are responsible for the bad name the entire bug family has in respectable society.

On the appearance and the habits of bed-bugs

Most of the bugs we have been talking about have wings and know very well how to use them. In bed-bugs the wings are mere remnants and of no use whatever. They have forgotten how to fly, and only because Nature is so very loath to drop old habits do we find that even today every new generation of bugs is equipped with rudimentary wings, though these do not grow with the bug but retain their stunted form as mere stumps (see figure on p. 44, adult bed-bug, magnified about 7 times).

They use their feet all the better. As they are interested in human beings only as a source of food, returning to their resting-places as soon as their appetite is satisfied, they just commute between their retreats and the bedsteads. They like to hide in cracks and corners of the bedstead, in the frames of pictures, in panelling or behind torn wall-paper. They attack sleepers, for they are fond of darkness and quiet. Since they generally take up their quarters near beds, no great strain is put on their marching powers. If hunger drives them, however, they can travel a considerable distance. Sometimes armies of them can be seen moving from an infested flat that the occupants have left. They will run along the outside walls in search of new hosts. If they are hungry enough, they forget their antipathy to light, and a neighbour may even find them entering his flat by an open window in broad daylight.

More often their invasion is unintentional, for bugs often get into houses with old furniture, picture-frames and other equipment or in clothing. And there are other opportunities for stowaways: their taste is by no means restricted to human beings, for they also attack cats and dogs, mice and rats, bats or rabbits. They also prey on starlings, sparrows and swallows, while hens and pigeons are often terribly plagued by these parasites. So coops for poultry or rabbits or deserted swallows' nests in the eaves often gain them entry into a house, though few will think of looking for the invaders in such places. Once indeed, bed-bugs were seen moving towards a house like tight-rope acrobats along telephone wires which were attached to an isolated dovecot.

If we look at the bed-bug's bill of fare we have just indicated, we see that their hosts always live in or near human habitations. Bugs seem to depend for food less on a particular kind of blood than on where their prey lives, a dependence which probably goes very far back. Since they have always been partial to warmth and dryness, they probably preyed even in prehistoric times on animals that had their resting-places in caves. Then prehistoric man arrived and improved the bugs' chances of life. From their standpoint, all the advances in our standard of living, from the simple hut to the all mod. con. flat of today, are merely improvements to the cave, whose essential features—dryness and uniform warmth—have been retained and intensified. And bugs have remained faithful to the atmosphere to which they were accustomed, except when cleanliness has kept them at bay.

Meals, social and family life

Bugs are fond of social life, though that takes different forms from human gregariousness. For us the dinner-table is a popular centre of sociability, whereas for the bugs meals are strictly private affairs. When feeding, it does not concern itself about its fellows.

As with fleas, both sexes of the bug are blood-suckers. The male bug is as a rule more slender than the female and not so greedy. While the female can absorb at one meal a quantity of blood equal to twice the weight of her body, the male takes at best only as much as his own weight. The fact that the proboscis or beak is so very fine makes it all the more remarkable that this quite considerable amount of blood can be sucked up in about ten minutes. The proboscis looks bulky because of its outer sheath, which bends at an angle when feeding is in process and does not pierce the skin. The following comparison may serve to show how fine the proboscis proper is: when a doctor injects a local anaesthetic or any other medicine into a patient, he uses a syringe, an instrument with a very fine, sharp, hollow needle. Instrument-makers try to make these needles extremely fine so that the puncture may be as painless as possible. Yet, the puncture made by the very finest needle is still more than 500 times bigger than the wound a bed-bug makes when it bites.

If bugs prefer solitary meals, they like plenty of company in their resting-places. Males and females, old and young, are often seen crowding together. All sizes and ages are represented, and young and old look alike except for the absence of the wing-buds on the former (see figure on p. 49), and the very youngest are pale in colour unless

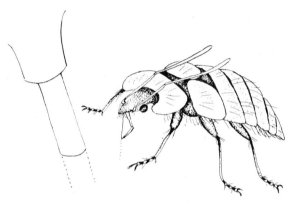

A bed-bug's proboscis is more than 500 times finer than the finest needle in a doctor's hypodermic. In the figure the proboscis is seen piercing the skin vertically, while the bulky sheath is bent backwards at an angle and does not pierce the skin (just as in the case of the gnat, see the illustration on p. 24). At rest, the proboscis lies in its sheath and is bent back, as may be seen in the lower left drawing on p. 49.

their skin is reddened by a recent meal of blood, which shines through the skin for a time. Flies lay their eggs in manure, gnats drop them on water, fleas let them fall into dust, and none of them pay any more heed to their brood. Have bugs a closer family life? Do they know anything about bringing up their young? No. There is not the slightest sign of any such thing. Their sociability consists merely in crowding together in suitable hiding-places, perhaps because they enjoy the smell of their kith and kin.

The expert can spot the bugs' hiding-places in an infested house by the typical smell given out by their stink glands and by the yellowish,

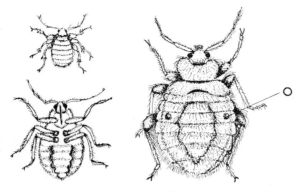

The larva of the bed-bug at three different stages of development: newly hatched, after the second moult, after the fourth
moult; it is mature after it has undergone five moults. The figure
of the second stage has been drawn from below in order to show
the position of the proboscis when at rest. O—organs with cells
containing bacteria, cf. pp. 52-53. (Magnified about 7 times.)

red-brown or black droppings that foul the woodwork or walls. It is
there, and in near-by cracks and crevices, that the females like to lay
their eggs. These are made fast by a sticky substance produced along
with the eggs, which hardens with exposure to the air.

In well-heated houses, bugs breed in winter, too. About three weeks

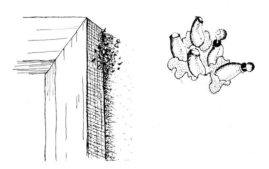

Excrement and eggs of the bed-bug; on the right a few eggs
(magnified about 7 times). They are firmly fixed to a surface by a
sticky substance.

after the eggs are laid, the young insects hatch. They are fully grown after about eight weeks and can then live and multiply for months, even for over a year.

There is one striking thing in this family chronicle which we have not mentioned so far: in the case of flies, gnats and fleas, the larva hatched from the egg is entirely different from the adult in shape and habits. When a larva is grown, it pupates and the fully formed insect emerges from the pupa. In this case, however, it is unmistakably a little bed-bug that creeps out of the egg. There is no pupal stage. The next section will explain this striking difference.

The art of jumping out of one's skin

When the tiny bug slips out of the egg, it is not laid in a cradle. It has the power to use its limbs from the very beginning of its life, and soon goes off in search of food. If it finds none, it can starve for two months. No new-born human baby could survive such conditions. In the bug world, however, as in that of other blood-suckers, a period of forced fasting may occur only too easily, and Nature has taken care to equip these infants with the necessary power of resistance. Of course, they cannot grow as long as they find no food; but one generous meal is enough to make them grow quite noticeably.

Like all arthropods, bugs have their growing pains. The outer case of chitin can only stretch to a certain limit. Like a too-tightly fitting jacket, it does not allow the body to expand much. Here the bug makes use of a method of self-help which as a rule has been proved efficient by all arthropods: it jumps out of its skin. It bursts its case of chitin and casts it. This is easier said than done, for in the process each of the insect's delicate legs must be drawn out undamaged. Moulting is always a critical moment and causes far more deaths than children's diseases do in our nurseries. If all goes well, the old skin, an exact impression of the body and its six legs, lies beside the moulted animal, which can expand for a few hours until the new coat-of-mail hardens.

This process is repeated five times in the life of a bed-bug before it reaches its final size. At least one meal of blood must be taken between every two moults. Since there are also tiny wing-buds on the mature animal, the latter differs very little from its larva. (Compare the adult bug illustrated on p. 44 with the larvae in the figure on p. 49.) This is not the case with the winged species of bugs, where the adult insect can be recognized at a glance by its fully developed wings, while the larvae in the first stage have no wings at all, and later only buds. There is a good reason why the wings should not be fully developed till after the last moult, for even the greatest skill in the art of moulting could not prevent a full-size wing from being damaged on its way out of the chitin sheath.

The moulting procedure adopted by bugs is also followed by grasshoppers, great numbers of whose tiny, and as yet unwinged, larvae can be found in the grass in spring, also by plant-lice and by many other insects. In their early stages the habits of such insects resemble those of the adults of their species, the chief change at the last moult being the fully developed wings. Such transformation can take place without any interruption of the life cycle. But in the case of the fly, the flea, the butterfly or the beetle, whose larvae are quite different in appearance and habits from the mature insect, things are different. Here, the shape and the internal organs must undergo such a complete change that the life cycle has to stand still for some time. This is the reason for the "pupa". Outwardly it is a period of rest but, inside, the organs of the larva are disintegrating and it assumes its ultimate shape. In the last moult the insect splits the pupa case and spreads its wings.

The wording of the last sentence recalls the old idea that pressure from the growing body bursts the skin, i.e. that moulting is a mechanical process. Recent investigations, however, have shown that the whole matter is not so simple, and bugs have supplied experimenters with excellent material.

It has long been known that vertebrates have certain glands which do not empty their products through ducts, as the salivary glands discharge saliva or the liver gall. The secretions of these ductless glands are emptied direct into the blood-stream which flows through the glands; so they pass with the blood throughout the body and as hormones have a great influence on the ordered course of vital processes. Our thyroid gland is such an example and is necessary for the regulation of growth. If the thyroid gland in a young person is removed, or if it is destroyed by illness, the development of his body and his mind suffers. There are many other "blood" or ductless glands, which must all work together in a complicated way if all the processes in a healthy body are to develop properly.

Until recently little was known about hormones in insects. That the moulting process is regulated by a definite hormone was first demonstrated by a simple experiment: the head of a bug (not a bed-bug, but a related species) was cut off. We should not survive such an operation, but it takes more than that to finish off a bug. It lives on without a head for many months and may even live longer than bugs with heads. But it does not moult again. Now there would be nothing surprising about a decapitated bug not being able to jump out of its skin. But if blood from a healthy bug is injected into it, moulting takes place quite normally, even in its headless state. Experimenters found that there is a tiny gland right beside the bug's brain and that the moulting process is caused by the product of this gland being emptied into the blood. The headless insect has lost this gland and so can only moult if it receives the necessary hormone from a healthy blood-donor. The most astonishing thing is that the hormone controls not only the time of the moult but the changes in the body connected with it. If the blood of older bugs is injected into younger ones that have not yet moulted for the last time, the latter are mature whenever they moult next. On the other hand, if ductless glands from larvae are transferred to adult bugs, these start moulting again and assume the characteristics of youth.

We shall not dwell longer on these learned details. Perhaps enough has been said to show that the results of such experiments have a meaning for life in general that extends far beyond the world of bugs. No animal is so insignificant that it might not reward our attention with great discoveries.

How the bugs get their vegetables

A wise mother sees that her family gets sufficient vegetables and fruit. That is good for them. Now we also know why. Such a diet is rich in vitamins—substances which are essential to life, although their importance was not recognized for a long time because they are present in food only in small quantities and are needed by the body only in small doses. But if our diet contains too few vitamins, or none at all, our health will suffer severely.

What has all this to do with bugs? We must remember that all living creatures are equal in the eyes of the great law of life: men are not superior to mice, nor bugs to men.

If we examine a bug under a magnifying glass, we shall see on either side of its intestines a small organ (marked O in the figure on p. 49) whose use is not at first sight apparent. It is neither a heart nor a gland, nor has it anything to do with either the intestine or the muscles. A very strong microscope reveals that its cells are filled with many living bacteria. Earlier references (p. 20) to these, the most primitive forms of vegetable life, as the causes of dangerous diseases have left unpleasant ideas about them behind. Bed-bugs unfortunately do not die from these bacteria, they do not even sicken because of them; on the contrary, they go into a decline if these bacteria are taken from them. The two organs we have just mentioned are there specially for the bacteria, their sole purpose being to provide them with a home and means of nourishment. Things have been so arranged that no bug is born without these bacteria; they are present in the mother-bug's body and find their way into the egg-cells, and later into the organs prepared for them during the growth of the bug's body.

Such an association with bacteria and other primitive vegetable forms is common in insects. It is known as symbiosis, by which term we understand a partnership of two different organisms living together for their mutual benefit. It is easy to see the benefit for the bacteria. They are provided with a suitable retreat where they can thrive excellently. And as they can be so providentially transferred from one generation to the next, there is no fear of their dying in the hard struggle for existence as long as there are bugs. How the bugs benefit has long been a puzzle. Why should a bug provide unbidden guests with free board and lodging among its intestines and arrange for them to be handed on to the next generation if it got nothing out of it? Observation and experiment have now led to the view that the bacteria are essential for the bug's nutritional requirements. They supply it with the vitamins necessary for healthy growth, just as we secure vitamins by eating fruit and vegetables.

Bed-bugs in electing to live on blood have chosen a very unbalanced diet, poor in vitamins. If we compare them with other blood-sucking insects, we recognize a remarkable law: if only the adults are blood-suckers while the young insects live on other material containing vitamins, no bacteria and no organs for these will be found, but where blood is the sustenance even of the larvae, symbiosis is always present. If vitamins were lacking for a whole life-time, the result would be disastrous. The habitats of the bacilli are like beds of vegetables where these blood-suckers unwittingly cultivate miniature vegetables as sources of vitamins.

This view is based on careful experiments and is well-founded. Yet many other unsolved riddles connected with symbiosis in insects still remain.

How can we get rid of bugs?

Some people never worry about insect bites. Not that they are particularly heroic. They just happen to react differently. A person may not feel gnat-bites at all and yet be greatly irritated by bites from a bug. Others again do not respond to bug-bites. A well-known entomologist once caught 890 bugs in one hour in a room in a Russian town, and thousands were still running about. Four other people sleeping in the same room declared unanimously that they had not noticed any bugs, and they certainly had not scratched themselves.

But these are exceptions, and most people prefer to sleep in a room free from bugs. Clearing a room of bugs is no easy task. It will be useless leaving it for some time in the hope of starving them out for adult bugs can fast for more than a year. A thorough search in all cracks and corners may yield a good "bag", but it will be impossible to discover all the bugs and their eggs. Nor does it help much to give the walls a thorough coating of paint. In one of his stories Gottfried Keller, the Swiss writer, describes how the hero goes to bed in his old room and how surprised and rather touched he is to watch a bug, reinvigorated by the warmth of spring, moving like a tiny blue mountain on the old, familiar wall which had been freshly painted several months previously. This has nothing to do with poetic licence, for similar observations are recorded in scientific books too.

Half measures are bound to be followed by a recurrence of the evil. The next section will show how vermin can be exterminated once and for all. Meantime, it would be best to have the infested room fumigated by an expert at the job.

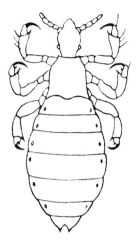

Lice

At the beginning of this book (p. 12) it has been stated that the art of flying comes naturally to insects. I am now in the rather embarrassing position of having to confess that lice cannot fly, any more than fleas or bugs can. There is not a vestige of wing-buds on their bodies. Yet I stand by my statement. It is because the insects just mentioned are parasites that they are an exception to the general rule. They need not travel far to find either food or mates. That is why their means of locomotion are so simple. Lice are not closely related to the bloodsucking insects we have been discussing up till now, nor even to their namesakes, plant-lice, which have much in common with bugs. Lice are in a class apart from other insects and have their own special order.

Various species of lice and their different preferences

To the human flea it is all one whether its host is a human being or a dog; it can be perfectly happy with either and is content on occasion with the blood of other hosts. We saw in the last chapter how varied the bug's bill of fare is; in comparison the louse is more particular about its diet. It confines its activities to men and apes. At the outset we should be clear that we cannot speak of "the" louse. Their order does not comprise as many species as that of the flea or the bug, but all the same we do know some 300 different species of lice. They live exclusively on mammals. The blood of birds, not to speak of lesser creatures, has no attraction for them. And in addition they follow strict rules with respect to mammals. One species lives on the stag, another on cattle, a third on mice, and there is a rabbit louse, a dog louse, a goat louse, a pig louse (though it will suck human blood too), even an elephant louse, which settles behind the ears of that huge animal and is an adept at piercing even its thick hide. We can almost say that every mammal has its own louse; and apparently every louse is convinced (if indeed it is possible to convince a louse) that its particular mammal is the only palatable one.

As a rule one mammal gets along with one species of louse. Man is an inglorious exception, for he can accommodate three species on his body: the head louse (illustrated on p. 55), the body louse (p. 59, lower illustration) and the crab louse (p. 59, upper illustration). They all drink the same blood, but not from the same tap. The head louse likes to live among the hair of the head, while the crab louse prefers the pubic region; the body louse may also be found in hair, but it is less of a local patriot than the others, and roams all over the body, a favourite haunt being the inner side of clothing, as its Latin name indicates (*vestimenti*).

The tenacity of lice

A head louse is neither winged like the gnat, nor has it the temperament and jumping powers of the flea. Not that it feels these deficiencies as it crawls sedately through the hairy undergrowth, for it has a special compensating equipment: strong claws on its feet (see illustration on p. 57) and powerful muscles which allow it to lock its claws and hold fast to the hairs. It just refuses to be dislodged. Nor does it leave the human body between "meals" in order to rest or to lay its eggs elsewhere. It attaches these eggs to the shaft of the hairs with a quick-setting substance which sticks like glue.

About two weeks later the young lice hatch out and leave the eggs ("nits"). Except for their size they are very like adult lice and have the same habits as these right from the start. That is why, like bugs, they can dispense with the pupal stage. After about three weeks they are fully grown and can breed without having to leave the forest of hairs on the head at all. Generations of lice can find accommodation on one and the same head. They are models of clinging tenacity, persistent hangers-on.

The claw at the end of the louse's foot is admirably adapted for hanging on.

And their bodies are well equipped to maintain their attachment. Their firm claws enable them to hold their ground even against heavy odds. With its forefeet alone a louse can carry up to two thousand times the weight of its body for a whole minute. This is more than the strongest athlete could ever hope to do; it would mean holding up a weight of 150 tons in his hands! The substance cementing the eggs to the hairs gives its young the same security and prevents the eggs from being detached.

The sense reactions of the louse are also in conformity with its sedentary habits. They seem to feel most comfortable when the thermometer stands at 28-30 degrees Centigrade. This personal detail was discovered by experimenting with what we call a "temperature organ". Imagine a longish passage divided into sections into which lice are herded. It is heated at one end and cooled at the other, with intermediate temperatures in between, so that the temperature falls throughout its length. Just as the pipes of an organ are arranged according to their length, the sections in the passage are graded according to their degree of warmth. The lice show a decided preference for the compartment with a temperature of 28-30 degrees Centigrade, which is obviously what they like best. Since they hanker after these conditions on the human body, too, they keep close to the roots of the hair, where the skin gives off warmth; they are safest there and also nearest their nourishment. And just because food is never far off, they do not over-indulge themselves as bugs and fleas do. They prefer to eat little but often, i.e. every few hours.

The head louse fastens its eggs (nits) to the hairs with cement that hardens.

In appearance and habits body lice resemble head lice very closely. We noted that they are to be found more frequently on other parts of the body than the head. They usually cement their eggs to the seams and rough surfaces of clothing rather than to hairs on the head and elsewhere. Crab lice differ in shape and are smaller. But they cling just as tenaciously to the thickets of hair where they have chosen to settle.

Annoying and dangerous vermin

Most blood-suckers carry their piercing mouth parts in a clearly visible sheath hanging down under their head. A louse's mouth looks quite harmless, showing neither sheath nor dagger, the latter being drawn far back into the head. It is extruded only at meal times. The food is sucked up in a few minutes. We know that lice are not hard drinkers; they treat themselves to small helpings of our blood at a time, but return for more all the oftener.

A crab louse. Middle and hind legs have powerful claws for holding on to hairs.

A body louse. Both, like the head louse on p. 55, are magnified about 20 times.

It is not the done thing to have lice. Indeed, personal cleanliness and better housing have generally tended to reduce their incidence. Regular checks by social and youth welfare agencies since the mid-sixties have, however, revealed an alarming increase in the occurrence of head lice. In part this may be due to a deliberate neglect of personal hygiene, partly to the longer hair styles favoured by young people which offer greater protection and cover to these insects. Because of their persistence, lice can multiply to an extent which can pose a threat to health.

On lice-infested heads lice are particularly numerous round the ears and on the hairs of the neck. They can even be seen clinging to the eyebrows and the beard. The bites itch so much that it is difficult not to scratch, thus causing wounds, which become easily inflamed if dirt gets into them. The discharge from them mats the hair, a condition that is furthered by the nits and their sticky cement. Where the hair is worn long, the result is a tangled mass, which is as difficult to straighten out as the legendary Gordian knot. The only thing to do is to cut the whole thing off.

In times of war, conditions in the field and in prisoner-of-war camps can provide lice with a particularly favourable environment. A well-known zoologist reported having removed in 1915 3800 body lice from the shirt of one Russian POW. In another case as many as 16,000 lice were taken off a badly neglected person.

However, if it had only been a matter of avoiding hair "mats" and sores produced by bites, less effort and money would have been spent on the battle against lice during the first world war. There was, however, something more serious at stake. A few weeks after the outbreak of the war, the German army on the eastern front became badly infested with lice. At the same time typhus wrought terrible havoc among soldiers and in prisoners' camps. Such epidemics used to be regarded as inevitable concomitants of war and no preventive measures were known. A short time before the war broke out, however, lice had been recognized as the sole transmitters of typhus fever. If there are no lice, there is no risk of infection for anyone who lives and sleeps in rooms where there are even dozens of typhus cases. Lice also carry other, less common, fevers and plagues (relapsing fever, trench fever, five-day fever, etc.). The best way to prevent such plagues from spreading is, therefore, to see that all lice are destroyed.

Gas warfare against lice and other parasites

To eradicate lice completely is easier said than done. Of course lice are not difficult to kill; with a little patience they can easily be found and caught. This is more difficult in the case of young lice since they are often too small to be seen; in the case of body lice with their habit of roaming all over the body, it is like looking for a needle in a haystack. Where several people are to be deloused, it is hopeless to try to catch every single louse. Infested bodies can be thoroughly cleansed with the help of chemicals. But how are clothes and underwear to be treated so as to kill every louse and destroy every egg? The application of the experience gained in gas warfare to anti-vermin measures was a great success. Poison gas is a most lethal weapon. It finds its way into all pockets and into the hidden folds of clothing; it is safe to use it also for things which would not stand up to treatment by steam or dry heat. After various gases were tried out it was decided that prussic (hydrocyanic) acid was best. During the first world war, as soon as the danger was realized, many cleansing centres were established. Such places had an airtight chamber in which clothing and other suspected articles were piled for treatment. If fumigation was carried out efficiently not a single louse-egg had any chance of surviving. People were only too glad also to smoke bugs out of hidden crevices in living-rooms.

Today this method, one useful product of the war, has been perfected. Since prussic acid must be used with great caution because it is highly poisonous for man, it has largely been replaced by less dangerous gases and gas mixtures. The expert must decide how best to proceed in individual cases and according to the vermin concerned, conditions in infested rooms, etc. Fumigation as a method of destroying vermin is now used to an undreamt-of extent. In flour mills, for instance, trouble is often caused by a small butterfly—the flour moth. Its tiny caterpillars live in flour; they not only feed on it and foul it with their droppings, but the threads they spin make it ropy. These lumps often clog the machinery and hold up work. So big mills have their entire plant fumigated at regular intervals, perhaps once a year, so that the pests never have a chance of surviving. Stocks of flour and other foodstuffs are not damaged, since the poison gas is so volatile that it disappears immediately if premises are aired for a short time. In cold storage plants, too, where rats and mice can be a great plague, the same method is often applied. Perhaps the greatest benefit derived from gas warfare was the extermination of rats on ships, a constant source of danger since they were feared as carriers of bubonic plague from overseas. The fumigation of big steamers is today a popular way of ridding them as radically and quickly of rats and other vermin as ever any Pied Piper could have done.

How one can get lice and how to get rid of them by methods other than those of gas warfare

If any reader imagines that lice have such good claws and are in all senses of the word so attached to their native quarters that they will stay where they are and certainly not emigrate, say, to his own head, he is mistaken. There are many reasons for such a change of quarters. Where the hair is thickly infested, lice like to take the air on ribbons, head-squares, or on the lining of hats. So all that is necessary is to put on one of those articles by mistake. Or one may lean without thinking against the upholstery of a railway carriage or a car and inherit lice from a less hygienic predecessor. In the same way direct contact with hair in crowds may lead to an infection.

Now, nobody will launch a poison gas attack because of a few head lice. Indeed it would scarcely be advisable to do so as long as they are on our heads. So we must look for a simple and safe home remedy. The recommended* modern insecticides for this purpose are malathion or carbaryl, which will kill not only the insects but their eggs as well. Available from chemists, they are marketed in the form of a lotion or shampoo and, if used according to the makers' instructions, will have a long-lasting effect.

Body lice, with their preference for settling in underwear and other garments except when they are feeding, have still more opportunities to change their quarters. Therefore all clothing in contact with lice should be boiled, steamed or dry cleaned. Materials which will not stand this should be exposed to dry heat (about 60-65 degrees Centigrade) for 30 to 60 minutes. A hot iron is quite good for this purpose.

*A leaflet on head lice can be obtained from the Health Education Council, 78 New Oxford Street, London WC1A 1AH.

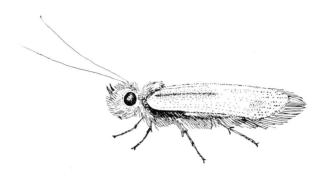

The Clothes Moth

However long winter lasts, the great day does come when we are sure that it has gone for good and when all winter clothing can be stowed away till next year. Wise housewives then have a busy time laying things in moth-proof storage.

Summer passes. Now and then a clothes moth flits through the room, a signal for much excited clapping of hands in a vain attempt to catch it. It may be brought low, or it just disappears, and the housewife wonders uneasily if her cellophane bags and sealed chests are really moth-proof. Autumn will show whether or not all her precautions—naphthaline balls and powder or newspaper wrappings—have been successful in preventing moths from gnawing ugly holes in the family's woollen garments.

Although the fact is generally known, I should like to repeat that moths do not make holes. Clothes moths are like butterflies. And butterflies have a fine, long tube, with which they suck nectar from flowers, but which would be of no use for gnawing a hole in a stocking. Moreover, clothes moths do not eat anything at all. They never break their fast during the months when they are in their winged state, and finally die of sheer weakness. This, however, does not exonerate them from blame in connection with moth holes, but it was away back in the caterpillar days of their youth that they were the culprits. Their progeny, if left to their own devices, will continue the work of destruction.

On butterflies in general and moths in particular

People often shake their heads sceptically when they hear someone asserting that clothes moths belong to the same order as butterflies. They connect the word butterfly with those brightly coloured marvels that are inseparable from the joys of their childhood—the Brimstones, Cabbage Butterflies, Red Admirals, Purple Emperors and all the rest of them. And the stouter, drabber specimens, the Owlet Moth and their like, which come in from the darkness outside and hover persistently round our lights, are generally acknowledged to belong to the same order. We know that out of the eggs of these butterflies caterpillars are hatched which develop a hearty appetite and pupate when fully grown. After a period of rest the butterfly emerges from the pupa.

It is the large butterflies that attract the majority of collectors, who of course know that the same order includes the huge army of micro-lepidoptera to which moths belong. These resemble their bigger relations in all essentials and there are species of intermediate sizes between these two groups. Up till now some 150,000 different lepidoptera have been identified, at least a quarter of them being micro-lepidoptera. There are several reasons why collectors are not as a rule interested in these smaller species. Many of them are so tiny that it is difficult to prepare and arrange them satisfactorily. Nor are they so easily classified as the big butterflies, not to mention that catching the latter is far more exciting and hence a greater delight. The connoisseurs who do not stop at small butterflies are rewarded by their great variety of shape, their marvellous colouring and the intricate veining on their wings, though it takes a magnifying-glass to reveal all their beauty.

Strictly speaking, the layman knows more about them than he himself suspects. Which of us has not sometime or other bitten into a worm-eaten apple? The reddish "worm" is the caterpillar of a very pretty, small butterfly. Another species is responsible for the "worms" in plums. We often see a curious pattern of wavy lines on the leaves of roses or other plants. Those underground passages are made by the tiny caterpillars of a leaf-mining moth, which are so small that they can eat their way inside a leaf, without damaging the upper or the under surfaces. The larvae live in the open on leaves and blossoms, as caterpillars usually do. It is not uncommon to find on fruit trees and various shrubs bundles of leaves and twigs bound together in a web of white threads; such webs conceal the larvae of the small ermine moth, a small butterfly with narrow, shining forewings delicately marked with black spots. So anyone who knows where to look will find moths and their caterpillars at every step. Most of them escape notice because they are so small and do not encroach on everyday life. But when the ermine moth makes for our fruit trees, when the flour moth gets into our flour, when the caterpillars of the grain moth wreak havoc in granaries, or when the clothes moth brings the housewife to the verge of despair, man puts up a stiff fight, employing all the means of destruction his superior reason can devise, though often enough they cannot prevail against the inexhaustible fecundity of his small opponents.

Things digestible and indigestible

The clothes moth, then, is a small butterfly. Most of its nearest relations, called moths in the narrower sense by zoologists, live in the caterpillar or grub stage on leaves, seeds and fruit, on things, that is, which are obviously nourishing. It must seem at least rather strange to the expert in human foodstuffs that the clothes moth should choose to live on fur and wool. We should neither enjoy nor thrive on such a diet. Not even if we were in the last throes of starvation would we bite into a bundle of hair. It would be of no use, either, since for us hairs are indigestible. What do we actually mean by "indigestible" and how can the caterpillars of moths exist on a diet of hairs? In order to answer those questions we must have a look at our insides and see what happens in the process of digestion.

The food we eat goes first into the stomach and then into the intestines. If it is to benefit the body it must pass through the wall of the intestine into the blood stream. That is possible only if it first dissolves in the watery content of the intestine. Many of our foodstuffs, sugar for instance, do so straight away; but when we eat bread or meat they must first be treated chemically and changed in order to be dissolved and then absorbed into the blood stream. This process is called digestion. It is brought about by "ferments" (enzymes), which are contained in the saliva, the gastric juices and in the secretions of the intestine, and which split foodstuffs up into simpler chemical compounds that are soluble in water. Different foodstuffs require different ferments. So whether we can digest a particular foodstuff will depend on whether our digestive juices contain certain ferments capable of breaking it down into its component parts.

Hairs originate in the skin. They are made of exactly the same substance as our finger-nails or as the uppermost layer of all the skin over our body or as a bird's feathers, a horse's hoofs or an ox's horns. The general name for this substance is horn. It is produced by the living cells of the skin undergoing a chemical change as a result of which they die off. It does not hurt to cut off nails or hair, for they are dead, and therefore insensitive, parts of the body.

Like the living cells from which horn originates, it consists of protein substances. Protein is an excellent food. We only lack the enzyme or ferment that can tackle, break down and dissolve this particular form of it. That is why we cannot assimilate either horn or hair. Now, the caterpillar of the clothes moth is equipped with such an enzyme and can subsist on hairs and feathers just as well as we do on meat and other protein foods. The bodily make-up of very few animals includes an enzyme which enables them to assimilate horny substances. We regard this property as strange just because it is rare, whereas we take the strangest things for granted when we experience them every day!

A scientist who was interested in the habits of moths made the following neat experiment: a patch of cloth woven from green cotton and red wool was left to moths. After some time green stains appeared on the patch, as the moths ate out the red wool and refused to touch the cotton. Cotton is a vegetable product. The lignin it consists of is chemically absolutely different from horn, which is an animal substance. Other enzymes are necessary to digest it and these are lacking in the clothes moth. That is why they cannot live on cotton.

Anyone interested in the more unusual phenomena of digestion will find just as much material for rewarding study in moths as in men. The clothes moth is not unique in this respect. There is, for instance, the wax moth, dreaded by keepers of bees for its devastating propensity for destroying the precious honey-combs. Wax, a fatty substance, is indigestible to moths. Yet in their intestines they harbour bacteria which can split wax into its digestible components. The larva of another species of moth lives on butter and also on the fat of dead animals or men. Even when the skeleton of an antelope is bleached by the sun of the African desert and when all the digestible parts of its carcase seem to have been devoured by marauders of all sizes, then a moth appears whose larvae gnaw the horns away; hundreds of pupae that cover the decaying horns are a proof that they have got what they wanted. So we get back to horn and to those who relish it. Quite a number of moth species are known in Africa and Asia which live in the caterpillar stage on horse-hoofs, buffalo-horns and the like.

Our clothes moths were of course compelled in Adam's day to search for their food in the open air. Today, too, in the outdoor world the skin and feathers of dead animals provide them with ample stores of food. Here clothes moths perform almost a useful job as scavengers. For what should otherwise happen to all the decaying hair and feathers which disintegrate so slowly? Such inexhaustible quantities of waste matter enable them to maintain their numbers in spite of the most dramatic measures employed to exterminate them indoors.

How moth holes are made

A mother moth does not take the trouble to fasten her eggs on to the hairs of wool or other material. She cannot manufacture cement as lice and bugs do. So moth eggs are easy to shake out of cloth. If they are left to develop in peace the tiny grubs hatch from the eggs after one or two weeks. If the cloth happens to be woollen and of the right quality, moths probably feel like cattle on rich pastures; and they set to work immediately.

There are different ways of doing everything. And so there are different ways of grazing. When the farmer drives his cows out to a fenced-off grass field and lets them roam at will over it, the grass becomes shorter. Tufts of herbage may be left standing, a sign that the cows do not find them to their taste; but no "moth holes" are eaten into the grass. The grubs of the moth do not graze uniformly over their wool pastures either. They tend to concentrate on one spot and—if they like the food—make such a hearty meal of it that in a thin material a hole can appear within twenty-four hours. The moths stay put for a good reason: they are building a home which they are loath to leave.

Caterpillars have spinning glands. They can produce a liquid thread from their mouths which hardens quickly in the air. Thus, the mature "worm" of the silk-moth spins a cocoon in which it pupates. Many

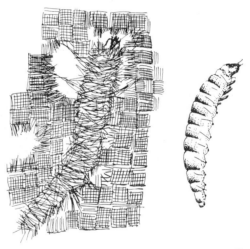

Caterpillar of a moth in its case. (*Right*) Side-view of a caterpillar removed from its case. (Magnified about 4 times.)

other butterfly caterpillars construct protective quarters for themselves in this way, for use during pupation. Small caterpillars can often be seen letting themselves down from a twig by a thread. This trick of spitting out a thread to be used like the climber's rope when they want either to make a lengthy descent to avoid danger or merely to change their abode might well be the envy of mountaineers.

As soon as the moth grubs are hatched they weave themselves a tiny tube to live in. They camouflage their home perfectly by covering it with bits of hair they have cut off, for the hairs are naturally the same colour as the material from which they have been removed. The grub need only push its head out of the tube in order to bite off and devour all the hairs one by one. In the case of fur, the grub has no objection to polishing off the dry skin too. When nothing is left within reach of the top of the tube, the home is extended a little. This of course is not done unless it is absolutely necessary, which explains why the feeding-places are so sharply defined.

The quiver-shaped tube not only prevents the delicate body of the grub from being seen and hurt; it has another important purpose. In woollen material there are no springs and no dew. The grubs of moths get nothing to drink all their lives. They must extract from their food all the moisture they require. Now, hair as daily bread is exceedingly dry. It is astonishing enough that the juicy grubs should be able to satisfy their liquid requirements from it. They have to be economical with their supplies of moisture. If they were exposed to the air they would be in

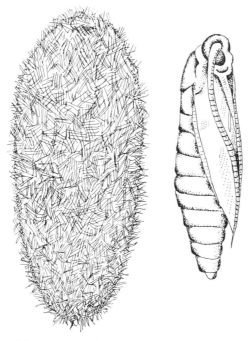

When fully grown, the moth caterpillar spins a case for itself (*left*) and changes into a pupa in it (*right*). (Magnified about 10 times.)

danger of shrivelling up. Just as bread is put in a bin to keep it from getting dry too quickly, so the caterpillars save themselves from giving off too much moisture by staying in the "bins" they have fabricated for themselves.

Home-loving though they are, moth caterpillars are, we must admit, not averse to roaming. When selecting a place for her eggs, the female moth is not very choosey. Whether it is because she cannot find anything better, or whether she is just too careless or unable to distinguish, she sometimes lays eggs on material that is not suitable for the grubs. Impelled by hunger, they leave their quivers and go foraging for food. Unfortunately Nature has not equipped them well for walking (see the caterpillar on the right of the figure on p. 68). The three pairs of short forelegs with their claws are just as little adapted for the purpose as the buds of the hind legs, particularly over the rough surface of cloth or fur. Here their ability to weave comes to their aid. When moving they never stop spinning, and fasten the thread to the cloth ahead of them, alternately right and left. So a silk ladder is formed of the many transverse threads and they can hang on to its rungs by their claws. This may be a cumbersome way of walking but they do advance and march gaily along at a speed of 40 centimetres an hour. When they eventually find better pastures, they settle down again.

The duration of the caterpillar stage depends largely on the quality of the food available. If it is suitable, from the moth's point of view, development may be complete after two to three weeks. If it is poor, it may take a year. When they are ready to pupate they move to a place from which the winged insect, when it emerges later, will have little difficulty in reaching the open air—for example, from the interior of upholstery to near the surface. They certainly do not know why they do this. It is the instinct of self-preservation, one of the thousands with which Nature has endowed the humblest of her creatures. Having reached the surface the caterpillars weave a fresh quiver, in which they pupate. After two weeks at the earliest the winged moth appears. If the weather is cold the pupal stage lasts much longer.

The retiring female

Moths are generally seen flying in the warm season of the year. In well-heated houses, however, they can breed all the year round. The number of eggs the female lays depends to a great extent on whether she was well or poorly nourished as a larva. On an average she lays about 100 eggs and takes about two to three weeks to do so. And this practically means the end of life as far as she is concerned. The male lives a few days longer.

What astonishes us is not that their life should be so short, but that it should be so long. For in their winged state they have only a vestigial mouth and intestines and are therefore incapable of eating or even of drinking throughout the weeks they live on the stores they have accumulated in their bodies as young caterpillars. And they draw to such an extent on their stores that when they die their bodies have only a half or a quarter of their original weight. With all their strength exhausted, life comes to a standstill, like a car that stops dead when the last drop of petrol has been used.

In many butterflies the sex can be distinguished at a glance. It is only the male of the Purple Emperor that is brilliantly coloured and the female Brimstone Butterfly can be recognized immediately by its pale, whitish wings; only the male Aurora Butterfly is marked with the beautiful orange-red spots. The male clothes moth is quite drab. Its narrow wings have the same dingy light-brown colour as those of the female. It must certainly have charms of its own to attract the female, but they must appeal not to sight but to another sense. It may be that it gives off a seductive scent that our noses cannot detect. Similar facts are known of other butterflies.

In one point, however, the male clothes moth is strikingly different from the female, and here I come to something that will lead to a disconcerting conclusion: the male often flies briskly about, whereas the female is averse to flying and generally hides in folds and crevices. It is little wonder that she is a reluctant flyer, for her egg-laden body is about twice as heavy as the male's but with only the same wing-span. When female moths are disturbed they scurry off in search of a fresh hiding-place. So when a lively moth flies round the room there is no point in the whole family chasing it. It is only a male. There are plenty of male moths, actually about double the number of females. So the birthrate will not be affected if a few more or less are killed. The female lies low; she does not often fly about voluntarily—a pity, since every female moth caught in good time means 100 eggs fewer.

Three kinds of moths

Before we launch a campaign against moths I must confess that I have omitted something: there is not just one clothes moth. There are three different species in our homes, which threaten our clothing, our carpets, upholstery and furs. The Clothes Moth proper (below, top illustration) is by far the commonest. A rare species is the case-bearing clothes moth, the "Fur" Moth (below, left) although it confines its attention just as little to furs as the clothes moth does to clothes. These

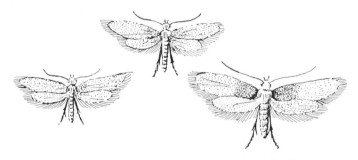

Clothes Moth proper (*top*), "Fur" Moth (*left*) and the Tapestry Moth (*right*). (Magnified about twice.)

two species can resemble each other so closely that most zoologists will find it difficult to distinguish them. The third species is the Tapestry Moth (right). I don't know where it gets its name from. At any rate its grubs also enjoy our woollen garments. The mature moths are easily distinguished from the other two species by the spotted wings, which are dark near the body. It won't be mistaken for a Clothes Moth by those who know anything about the latter. Those who do not know the difference and who kill indiscriminately every small butterfly they can catch in the house—to the sorrow of the butterfly-lover—may also catch a Tapestry Moth. It won't matter much, for it will very probably be a male.

Now that I have unburdened my zoological conscience we may disregard distinctions, since the same measures of moth control may be applied in dealing with all three species.

Moth control

In his fight against moths man has an ally which is not widely known: a small ichneumon-fly. It hunts out the young moth caterpillars, pierces their bodies and lays an egg in each. This egg hatches inside the caterpillar into a grub-like larva, which gradually eats up its host from within. At first it spares the caterpillar's vital organs so that they may continue to function for the benefit of its parasite. When the caterpillar has completed its growth, the larva of the ichneumon is almost the same size. Then the caterpillar's last hour has come. The cocoon it manages to spin is at the same time a coffin for itself and a cradle for its parasite.

Many moths also fall victims to spiders and other enemies. But there are also many left and the housewife must take measures to protect her possessions against them.

The old custom of brushing and beating articles that may be attacked and airing them helps a lot. For the caterpillars shun warmth and light and will abandon their cases if disturbed even slightly. The brushing, however, should not be done indoors, otherwise the homeless caterpillars will find fresh pastures in other articles and the result will be more moth-holes than before. Moths can also be destroyed by carefully ironing the cloth they have attacked with a hot iron.

Another common protective method is to wrap clothing, etc. in newspaper. We have no proof that moths are averse to printer's ink, so it does not matter whether the wrappings are of printed paper or not. If only they are thick and have no openings whatever, no moth will get in since it cannot eat its way through paper. Provided there were no eggs or caterpillars on the articles, paper wrappings will keep them safe. To this fact we owe the moth-bag, an excellent invention.

There are many chemical moth-balls and powders, made mainly of naphthalene, camphor and similar compounds. They are not only preventives but, if used in sufficient quantities, they destroy the moths themselves as well as their eggs and caterpillars. To be effective, they must be generously applied, and articles thus treated must be well wrapped in paper or something similar and stored in a box, which should then be hermetically sealed to prevent the chemicals from escaping. Some preparations must be renewed every three or four weeks.

The chemical industry has discovered a more effective means of moth-protection, which has proved better than all these older methods: to treat materials in such a way that they can never be attacked by moth caterpillars. This is best done while the material is being manufactured. Impregnation with eulan is the best-known method and it has stood the test of time. Material thus treated is moth-proof. If eggs are laid on such cloth and young caterpillars begin to crawl about, they soon die. Strips of card impregnated with lindane have proved their worth in wardrobes and drawers. They should be renewed from time to time, monthly to be on the safe side. Aerosol sprays are also effective.

But until the contents of wardrobes and drawers are moth-proof, down to the last stocking, the war on the domestic front against moths will not be won.

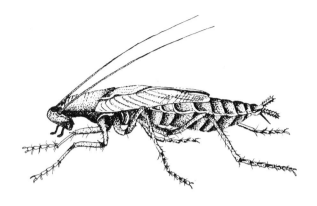

The Cockroach

To the zoologist cockroaches are insects which are closely related to grasshoppers and crickets. They are just as unpopular as clothes moths but differ in all other respects from them as much as a green grasshopper does from a butterfly.

A community that has come down in the world

The cockroaches of antiquity were very similar to those of today. Masses of them lived in the dense thickets of ferns and horsetail grass in the shade of the luxuriant vegetation which in due course formed deposits of coal. They are among the most primitive of living insects, whose ancestry goes far back in history to a time when there were no flies, bugs or butterflies. The amber flea with its 40 million years is a mere stripling compared with those cockroaches, many fossils of which have been found in deposits estimated to be 280-300 million years old. A span of even 300 years sees marked changes in the habits and customs of human society, and yet a period of 300 million years was not long enough to make any difference to the cockroach's preference for the twilight of the humid, dark forest. The giant ferns and tree-like horsetail grass have disappeared. But the greatest number of all known cockroaches still inhabit tropical forests, an environment in which

75

living conditions probably resemble those produced by the primeval flora most closely. In the temperate zones they are comparatively rare. A few species have become housemates of man. They have learnt to invade houses, being fond of places that are dark and humid. It may be that such places stir in them memories of their ancient home in primeval forests. They thrive best in kitchens, bakeries, breweries, warm larders and hothouses. They shun the light and hide by day behind cupboards and chests, pictures and panelling, in cracks and crevices round sinks and heating pipes, waiting till it gets dark before they come out in search of food. They fall on everything that is palatable, though naturally the cockroach's taste is not necessarily ours. They have been known to eat not only potatoes and vegetables, bread and chocolate, sugar and honey, fat and all mannner of garbage, fresh and decayed, but also paper, ink and shoe-polish, though the latter items could scarcely be of much benefit to them. When food is good and quarters comfortable they multiply tremendously. They then become a real domestic plague, not so much because of the stores they consume as because of their unsavoury habits. They crawl over everything, steal everything and foul everything with their droppings, and they give off a nasty smell. They have special glands which emit what may be a pleasant perfume to their organs of smell. If they are disturbed in their secret feasting, they scurry off to their hiding-places, making a rattling noise that can give timid people a bad fright.

Compared with their cousins who live in forests these parasites seem to us to be a somewhat degenerate, but nevertheless thriving, community. Transported by men with their household goods, they have invaded practically all countries. They can be brought into even the cleanest house by mere chance. They are not popular anywhere, as is seen in Germany from the names given to them in various localities. In many places in South Germany they are known as "Prussians", in the North as "Swabians", in West Germany they are called "Frenchmen", in the East "Russians". In Russia they are again "Prussians". Evidently one's closest neighbours have always been blamed for their appearance.

Appearance and habits

In addition to the common cockroach another species, the German cockroach, is frequently met with in Germany. We cannot help thinking that even scientists have not been without the patriotic prejudices we have just indicated. For it was the famous Swedish naturalist, Carl von Linné, who gave the name of *Phyllodromia germanica* to this species, although it is by no means confined to Germany but is found in all the countries of the civilized world and even in the most primitive and remote of human settlements.

The German cockroach. (*Left*) A male; (*right*) a female. (Twice their natural size.)

The mature cockroach is a little longer than 1 centimetre and is light brown in colour.

The oriental cockroach (*Blatta orientalis*) is also called the black beetle. It grows to twice the size of the German cockroach and is dark, almost black. The female of this species, even when fully grown, has only rudimentary wings, whereas the wings of the male are fully developed. American cockroaches are less common in our part of the world. They were first noticed in Europe in big ports, having obviously come over from America as stowaways. They are of course bigger than our common cockroaches. In the forests of South America there are species as long as a finger. Let us hope they will stay there!

If looked at closely, cockroaches are neat little creatures. Their two long antennae, thread-like and mobile, stand them in good stead when they have to feel their way quickly through a dark room. The head has a different appearance from that of other insects; it has, one is tempted to say, the lofty brow of a philosopher! (Illustration on p. 75.) There is, however, probably not much behind it, for the brain is small. The flatness of its body enables the cockroach to penetrate into cracks, its favourite haunts.

They seldom use their wings and only for short distances. On the other hand, they often bring themselves to make short jumps, a habit in which their long-legged cousins, the grasshoppers, have become champions. Cockroaches are best at running. They can sprint at a speed of 1 kilometre an hour, which of course does not mean that they can progress at this rate for an hour on end. They tire too quickly, and moreover, they do not need to have such staying powers. It only takes them a few seconds to reach their hiding-places, where they can recover from their exertions. Nature is not recklessly extravagant in dispensing her gifts and has only endowed those of her creatures with a capacity for endurance if it is essential for the preservation of their life.

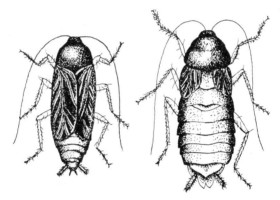

The oriental cockroach. (*Left*) The male; (*right*) the female.
(Twice their natural size.)

When the female lays her eggs she packs them in a hard, durable case. This is done automatically, not deliberately. As every egg leaves the ovary it is enveloped in matter secreted by glands, which harden rapidly till a big, firm ball is formed, each egg lying neatly in its own compartment. The common or oriental cockroach deposits its egg ball or capsule after a few days, that is, it just lets it drop and troubles no more about it and its contents; the German cockroach is not so happy-go-lucky: it carries the capsule around, attached to its abdomen, for three or four weeks, till the eggs are ready for hatching. Then the capsule drops, splits lengthwise, and the way into the wide world lies open to the young cockroaches.

Except that they have no wings, the larvae resemble their parents even in the first stage. They are at first so tiny that they can gain access to fresh territory through a hole 1 mm wide and 0.5 mm deep. So such a minute crack is big enough to enable these unwelcome visitors to enter a clean house.

Common cockroach depositing its egg capsule.

Cockroaches moult six times before they reach maturity. Since we have come across this process already we need not describe it in detail. From the biological facts we are already acquainted with, we should not expect a cockroach to go through a pupal stage, and it would be useless to look for one. From the start the larvae have the same habits as the adults; but for the missing wings, their bodies have the same shape and no great transformation is necessary. After the last moult the wings grow quickly to their full size, and development is thus complete.

During the moults one of the long, delicate legs or some other part sometimes catches and is damaged by the sharp edges of the chitinous skin that has been cast. Trivial though such an accident may seem, it may have very serious consequences. For the greed of cockroaches knows no bounds. They have no objection to licking the blood of a near relative and once they have tasted it, they cannot stop until they have gobbled up their victim alive. Such cannibalistic habits may be of importance in maintaining the vigour of the species, since they ensure the elimination of weak and diseased members. Their practice of eating cases of quite sound eggs, which they often do, is inexcusable. Householders will naturally not protest. It is only a pity that such a habit has little influence on the fecundity of these creatures. They breed continuously in warm houses, even in winter.

The benefit of chewing

It is related of John D. Rockefeller that he wanted to live till he was a hundred and that, in order to achieve his aim, he used to spend a long time chewing his food very thoroughly. This may sound odd, but the idea behind it is absolutely sound. The digestive juices can act far better on well-masticated food than on solid lumps. It can then be assimilated more quickly and thoroughly. This is important for our general efficiency, since food is the source of all the energy we require for physical labour or mental activity.

It is natural for us to chew a piece of bread before we swallow it. A glance at the entire animal kingdom shows that the ability to chew is actually a rare gift. It is true that the pike's mouth is full of teeth, but they are sharp cones, pointed backwards, not adapted for biting up its prey, but only for preventing its escape. The frog gulps its flies down whole, and the giant snake similarly swallows a pig at one go. Of the vertebrates only the birds and the mammals grind down their food mechanically, the former by means of the grinding-stones in their gizzards, the latter with their teeth. It is no mere chance that the birds and the mammals should be warm-blooded creatures with an active metabolism, energetic, and ahead of other vertebrates in mental ability too.

The same phenomenon can be observed among the lower animals. Such insects as do not live on liquid food are able to chew, and it is not fortuitous that they are superior to all the other lower animals in agility and general efficiency.

John D. Rockefeller might have envied the cockroach. It chews its food, not only with its mouth but, after the food is swallowed, with its stomach too, this organ being equipped for chewing with sharp, hard, chitinous teeth and strong muscles. Ingenious though this invention is for completing the mechanical process of breaking down food, it is nothing compared with the imagination Nature has displayed in the structure of the cockroach's mouth-parts. They are marvellous enough to make it worth while spending a little time on them.

Mouths that bite, lick, suck and sting

When we bite, our lower jaw must meet our upper jaw, which is immovably fixed in the skull. The insect's biting processes are much more complicated. Perhaps to some extent this is a sign that insects are on a lower level of development than we, just as an old iron bridge, with its many supports and buttresses, may seem to be a clumsy and imperfect structure compared with a modern bridge. Yet the very variety of an insect's mouth-parts gives them evolutionary potentialities which vertebrates can never possess.

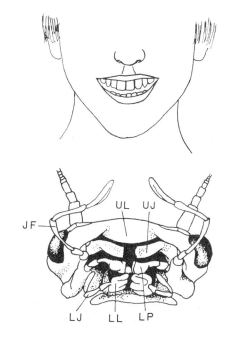

In man the lower jaw moves upwards to join the upper jaw; insects work their jaws from left to right. The lower drawing is a greatly magnified illustration of the mouth-parts of the cockroach. UL= upper lip, UJ=upper jaw, LJ=lower jaw, JF =jaw feeler, LL=lower lip, LP= labial palp (lip feeler).

We ourselves and all our kind move our jaws upwards when we bite. But there are different ways of doing the same thing. Insects bite from the right and the left. Cockroaches have very powerful jaws set with strong teeth of chitin. Chewing goes on in front of the mouth cavity. They have a flap of skin which covers the bite like an upper lip and prevents it from slipping out. Behind the first pair of jaws there is a second pair. The first pair, relatively simple and strong in structure, are employed when brute force is needed, whereas the second can be used in so many ways that in comparison, our own jaws can only be described as a clumsy, unimaginative device (cf. the left illustration of the figure on p. 83). Sharp, finer teeth at the outer ends of this jaw serve to sever bits of food and push them towards the mouth; the folded part in the middle is covered with bristles and, along with another appendage, acts as a little brush which serves the purpose of cleaning feelers and legs when they are dusty; in addition, these parts have a jointed appendage (the maxillary or mandible palp), equipped with numerous sensory organs in the shape of hairs; they feel the bite while it is being "dressed" and check it for taste. After the second, extremely mobile, pair of jaws follows a thick lower lip, which prevents any of the food from falling out, and that, too, has appendages covered with sensory organs (labial palps).

In spite of their complicated structure such mouth-parts are regarded by experts as primitive and comparatively simple forms. All insects which have come down to us from the Carboniferous Age as fossils belong to species with such biting mouth-parts. In later periods of the earth's history new groups of insects appeared with specialized habits of eating. All who are interested in the evolution of the different forms will be struck with astonishment and admiration at the way mouth-parts are transformed into specialized instruments, very limited in use, but highly finished in form.

In wasps, for instance, the upper lip and the first pair of jaws have retained their original form and function, but the second pair of jaws and the lower lip have been lengthened and combined to form a movable little brush for collecting honey and other liquids. In bees (see centre figure on p. 83) these parts have been further lengthened and modified into a proper sucking tube. In gnats (cf. figure on right) all the mouth-parts have been greatly lengthened and attenuated. The upper lip has been extended and its edges rolled in to form a thin sucking tube, then come the two pairs of jaws, transformed into the finest piercing bristles dotted with tiny teeth, the "jaws" being movable up and down. The lower lip, which does not pierce the skin, serves as a guide (cf. illustrations on p. 24).

The comparative study of forms, of whose richness our few examples can give but a faint idea, has led to the conviction that in spite of the

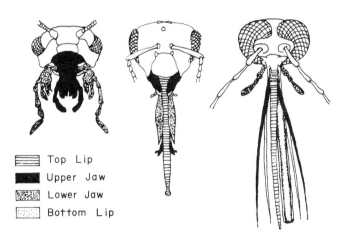

◼ Top Lip

◼ Upper Jaw

◼ Lower Jaw

◻ Bottom Lip

(*Left*) The biting mouth-parts of a cockroach. (*Centre*) The sucking mouth-parts of a bee. (*Right*) The piercing mouth-parts of a gnat (mosquito). Corresponding parts are shaded in the same tone. The adaptation to special functions is based on an extensive transformation of the primitive mouth-parts. Of the feeler located on the front of the head only the segments near the body are shown.

differences in their appearance, all the mouth-parts of insects are derived from those of the most primitive of their ancestors and have been gradually adapted in the course of time to the foods of the different species. It is a small, but very illuminating example of the transformation all forms of life have undergone in the course of the development of species. Every naturalist probably has his own opinion as to what forces were involved, but no one ever looked over the shoulder of the Creator when he was working on the creation of living creatures, and no man knows exactly how it has been done.

Cockroach control

Wherever cockroaches are in evidence, steps should be taken to get rid of them. The measures adopted will depend on whether they are merely a nuisance or a serious menace. In the home every effort will be made to exterminate such unsavoury propagators of filth. Cleanliness and the prompt removal of food remnants and kitchen garbage will help a lot. Cockroaches only settle where they find food and harbourage. If they have managed to do so, the extent of infestation should be determined by inspection at night and a spray of either propoxur or dioxacarb be applied. In hot or dusty places boric acid powder can be used.*

Cockroaches sometimes cause such damage that their eradication calls for costlier and more complicated measures. In libraries, for instance, they sometimes eat their way through valuable book-bindings, probably tempted by the glue, or they sometimes gnaw off the gold letters on the backs of leather-bound books in order to get through to the albuminous paste behind. In hospitals they are dangerous housemates, since they have been proved to carry the germs of disease both internally (in their intestines) and externally (on their legs). In such cases fumigation is recommended, a process we have already mentioned as being the most effective method of rendering a building vermin-free after one operation only.

*For further details see Advisory Leaflet 383, Ministry of Agriculture, Fisheries and Food (Publications), Tolcade Drive, Pinner, Middlesex HA5 2DT.

Aphids (Plant-lice)

What, more lice? Yes, but these have nothing to do with head lice or other blood-suckers, they are plant-lice—aphids or greenflies. Show me the gardener or owner of house-plants who hasn't come across them. When spring arrives he notes with distaste their appearance on the fresh green shoots of the elder and other shrubs, on the new growth on the apple trees, and particularly on his budding roses. At first there will be just a few of them here and there, but very soon they can become so numerous as to cover the entire plant stem. House-plants fare no better. That's when the aphids become housemates of ours and give us the chance of studying them at leisure. As if anyone would want to, you might say. Nevertheless, it is generally known that if badly attacked by these aphids plants will wilt and buds wither; that they can carry harmful plant viruses will probably also be common knowledge. It is usually thought advisable, therefore, to pick these insects off the plants—and a thoroughly messy business it generally turns out to be. Their soft bodies are easily squashed, leaving a sticky pulp on one's fingers. Moreover the process is rarely effective since the young insects, being exceedingly small, are easily overlooked and can rapidly make good the losses inflicted upon them. But that is not the only noteworthy aspect of their existence, so let us take a closer look. We might even discover afterwards how best to get rid of them.

Over 3000 different species of aphids (*Aphidina*) have been identified. Some resemble each other so much that even the expert will be hard put to it to tell them apart and even he might have to observe their whole life cycle before being able to make a positive identification. Very often a particular aphid's life cycle is more of a characteristic than its appearance. This in fact varies tremendously. Rather than go into all the details, which would lead us away from our main subject, let us just deal with a simple example and thereby get to know the whole family.

The rose fly and its many children

Macrosiphum rosae—the large rose fly—may be its scientific name, but "large", being a relative term, here merely means that it may attain a length of 2-3 millimetres. In general, aphids are tiny, delicate insects which cannot withstand the rigours of our winter without protection. They survive the cold weather as overwintering eggs that are enclosed in a tough shell and have been produced by that year's last generation of females. As soon as the roses begin their spring growth, each of these eggs will hatch a female which in its turn will become the progenitor of a whole series of rose fly generations.

The greenfly on our rose tree draws its food from the sap of the new shoots, using for the purpose its piercing and sucking mouth-parts. So wholesome is the diet that it will mature in 10 days and will then be ready to multiply. Despite several moults, its outward appearance hardly changes, except for size, nor does it develop wings. Not that it will need them—after all, it will find everything it requires to hand. No males will appear at first: their presence is not really necessary for the eggs develop in the females' ovaries without fertilization. This development of an embryo from an unfertilized egg is called parthenogenesis or virgin birth. It is responsible for an almost explosive increase in the aphid population, firstly because every single insect can produce offspring and secondly because, since the embryonic development of the eggs begins very early, i.e. in the mother's infancy, the young are born almost fully-fledged as soon as the female has reached maturity (figure below). These young aphids, or nymphs, which are still almost exclusively female, continue to multiply by partheno-genesis and a speedy succession of generations of this kind means that a single greenfly can give rise to a sizeable colony of offspring (figure on p. 88). Incidentally, giving birth to fully formed young, or viviparity, is quite a widespread feature among insects and in the animal kingdom as a whole.

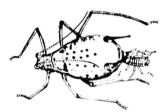

Birth of an aphid.

Watching the growth of the greenfly population on his roses with new-found interest and, it is hoped, some understanding, the reader may well wonder how on earth all these new generations of offspring could possibly be accommodated on the host plant. To his surprise he will discover that, as the generations follow one another, a winged form of aphid makes its appearance alongside the wingless variety. The flighted type develops thin-skinned wings which shelter the equally delicate body like a roof when it is at rest. In calm weather it will take to the air and may then land on another rose bush where it will promptly found a new colony. Its departure also helps to reduce congestion on its former host-plant. True, many a traveller will never reach his destination, but no matter, there will always be plenty of others to take his place.

As summer passes, as many as 10 parthenogenetic generations may appear. With the arrival of autumn, the first male aphids will come on the scene in addition to the females. The latter can now no longer

Elder fly colony (*Aphis sambuci*). Fully developed aphids and nymphs completely cover the plant's stem. Ants benefit from the supply of honeydew.

multiply by parthenogenesis but have to rely on sexual reproduction. Eventually these females will produce the hard-shelled overwintering eggs mentioned earlier. Thus the annual cycle is closed.

Although the aphid might content itself with a life on our roses all the year round, it will occasionally change to other plants, e.g. scabious. Some species of aphids—generally not found in our homes or gardens—will always attack a specific plant. Far more often, however, a species will have to abandon the plant which has been its involuntary host for another in order to be able to complete its life cycle. Such a host shift occurs in our next example.

The black bean aphid

The aphid on our roses may be green or reddish in colour: that is immaterial, being just a case of sisters wearing different colours. The black bean aphid (*Aphis fabae*), usually known as blackfly, is as its name indicates black.

Again starting with spring, as the beans have not yet come through, the overwintering eggs cannot be found on them but are located on other plants, such as the spindle-tree (*Euonymus europaeus*), which acted as their winter host. The parthenogenetic first generation of blackflies, therefore, will be feeding on the green shoots of this plant. Yet, as soon as the second generation is hatched, a considerable number of winged insects will appear, ready to fly off in search of field, broad, French or runner-beans, which will be their favoured summer host, although they will also settle for poppies or other plants. In any case, they will have left the spindle-tree by May for the very good reason that its sap flow will have diminished and become less nutritious: so off they go in search of lusher pastures on the beanstalks, where—once established—they will multiply at a massive rate.

In the autumn the time has come for the return journey to the spindle-tree: the winged females now leave their summer quarters for the leaves of the winter host. There they produce—still partheno-genetically—the wingless females that will eventually be fertilized by the males. At that time, the latter are still being born on their summer host; they develop wings there, thus enabling them to join the females on the spindle-tree early in October. Mating can now take place and the resulting overwintering eggs invariably ensure an ample supply of blackflies in the coming year.

Incidentally, one might ask whatever makes these aphids, after so many generations of asexual reproduction, produce suddenly, and as if by previous arrangement, males, and go in for sexual reproduction? It was found that the change is prompted by external circumstances, i.e. by the shortening days of autumn and by the lower temperatures. The black bean fly furnished conclusive evidence of this. For no less than 16 years a blackfly colony was kept continuously in an artificial environment which simulated the long days and short nights of summer at a temperature of 18-20 degrees Centigrade; during this entire period over 700 generations were produced parthenogenetically and without the appearance of a single male. By contrast, a lowering of the temperature and shortening of day-length triggered off the sexual reproduction process even in mid-summer.

When aphids go a-journeying

We have said that in certain circumstances aphids will abandon their host plant for another. This plant is often of the same species, such as when greenflies leave an overcrowded rose tree and settle on another close by, attracted no doubt by the colour of its leaves. Flights of this type are undertaken only in the most favourable conditions: the air has to be dry, warm and still, for even the lightest of breezes would blow this small-winged insect way off course.

Where longer distances are involved, the journey becomes far more hazardous. Not every row of beans can be expected to have a spindle-tree within easy reach. A lengthy expedition may therefore be necessary, a journey moreover on which the blackfly will not have the benefit of modern navigational aids. Often it will rise to a considerable height and be carried many miles by air currents before coming down again in calmer conditions. These long-distance trips promote the distribution of the species over a wide area as proved by experiments with radioactive tracers. Wherever the insects come to earth, they must find a suitable plant to settle on. This is done by trial and error: mostly the foliage to which they have been attracted will prove to be of the wrong kind. As a rule they realise this after a quick preliminary probing lasting no more than a minute and move on without taking any food. Often, however, they will be obliged to taste the food, i.e. pierce the leaf and suck some of the plant juices. Unless this test is satisfactory, they retract their proboscis and take off again to try their luck elsewhere. This tasting process may last up to an hour or more. No wonder the large majority of blackflies never arrive at their proper destination. The outlook would indeed be bleak for them but for the improvement in their chances of survival thanks to their enormous fertility. In this the process resembles wind-blown pollination where, because of the huge numbers of pollen involved, fertilization will always take place with some degree of certainty.

The development of the different species of aphids may vary in a hundred details, but these are best left to the expert; instead, let us look at exactly what happens when an aphid pierces a plant stem, what is being absorbed, and how the food is used.

Aphids as sugar producers

If a gnat or flea wants to help itself to some of our blood, it can do so anywhere on the skin thanks to the pervasive network of capillaries, as any pinprick will show. Although no blood may course through a plant, it does have a well-developed internal vascular system. This consists of tubes made up of straight, elongated and microscopically thin cells, often grouped in vascular bundles (figure below). The tissues on the

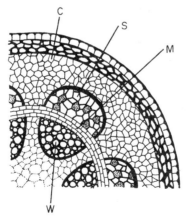

Transverse section of plant shoot showing radial arrangement of vascular bundles. W= water-carrying tubes; S=sieve tubes; C=cortex; M=cell-producing tissue (Meristem).

inside of the bundles conduct the water absorbed by the roots upward
to the leaves, whereas the channels on the outside carry the organic
substances synthetized in the plant, especially sugar, to the parts where
they are needed or where they will be stored. These latter conduits are
called sieve tubes because the end walls of their elongated cells are
perforated and communicate through "sieve-plates" with the adjoining
cells. It is these sieve tubes the aphids are after: but how do they get at
their content?

The sucking proboscis contains two pairs of slender lancets or stylets
which will be driven into the green shoot, while the thick outer covering
is folded back like a sleeve. The way the proboscis penetrates the plant
tissue is a remarkable process. Whenever plant cells with tough,
cellulose walls obstruct the passage, the proboscis will seek to wind its
way between the cell walls, using the enzyme of its saliva to dissolve the
binding substance between the cells. So, to get round the individual
cells, the proboscis must by-pass them and the ingenious way in which
it is constructed enables it to perform this side-step. The two inner
stylets are loosely joined to each other and can alternately be pushed
forward; muscles located at the base of the proboscis can also bend
them sideways. In addition, while the proboscis is being lowered further
and further, the aphid dribbles its quick-setting saliva down it, thereby
creating round the puncture canal a hard-walled tube that secures the
channel and keeps it open along its entire tortuous path. As soon as the
proboscis meets a sieve-tube it pierces it and gains access to the sugary
sap (figure on p. 93). Having done so, the aphid, with no good reason to
move, now stays put.

Though an aphid would be quite capable of sucking the sap through
its proboscis, as a rule there is no need for it to do so for generally the
sap is under pressure in the sieve-tube and this will make it rise through
the proboscis of its own accord. Proof of this is furnished by severing
the head from the body while the insect is feeding: the sap will be seen
continuing to flow through the dismembered head and proboscis for
2-4 days. At times the flow to the stomach must even be stemmed by the
insect, for if prevented from doing so, e.g. by being anaesthetized, it will
simply burst.

Now, it is essential to realize that a living organism cannot be built
from carbohydrate food alone. Proteins are needed, and in these

substances, or rather in the amino-acids which are the bricks from which proteins are made, the plant juices are deficient: they are present in far smaller quantities than is sugar. Hence, to obtain all the necessary building materials for their rapid growth, the aphids must take in huge quantities of sap, thereby supplying their intestines with far more sugar than they can absorb. The excess is excreted unchanged.

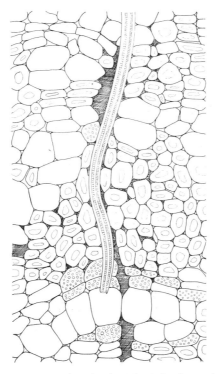

Part of transverse section of a plant shoot showing proboscis of an aphid which has just pierced a sieve-tube. Greatly magnified.

This substance is called honeydew and whenever a droplet passes through the aphid's anus a strong contraction of the colon flicks it some distance clear of the insect, thereby ensuring the cleanliness of the immediate surroundings. Where aphids occur in large numbers, e.g. in conifer forests, whole areas may become coated in sugar. Beekeepers are usually delighted when this happens and take their hives to these patches. The resulting "forest honey" is highly prized for its subtle flavour. People are generally taken aback when they learn that the delicacy they have enjoyed comes from the excreta of plant-lice. Yet there is really nothing distasteful about it: what has passed through the system of these insects is only pure plant juice.

Apart from honey-bees, other insects with a "sweet tooth", such as wasps and ants, will also be attracted to these sugary patches. Ants, as we shall see later, develop a particularly intimate relationship with aphids (see pages 108-10).

Enemies of the aphids

Aphids are ill-equipped for a quick get-away as their spindly legs are not much good for running or jumping. So a colony of aphids can easily become a feeding-ground for other insects. The ladybird (*Coccinella septempunctata*), probably the most frequent visitor of these infestations, is perhaps also the greenfly's worst enemy: it can gobble up to a hundred a day.

The ladybird's larva, too, finds aphids to its taste. Hoverflies (figure on p. 95), amazing aerobatic performers that can suddenly stop in mid-air while beating their wings and disappear in a burst of speed in the twinkling of an eye, may prefer to feed on blossoms, but their larvae are active predators and great exterminators of aphids. The minute ichneumonid wasp deals with its prey in yet a different manner: the female punctures the aphid and lays its eggs inside it (figure on p. 96). Subsequently the aphid will be devoured from the inside by the parasitic larva until nothing but its skin is left. In the meantime the larva has matured, pupated, and emerges eventually as a small wasp, still small enough to find accommodation inside its victim. Many other insects that are after the greenfly could be listed: with their soft bodies and large numbers, aphids almost seem to invite their enemies' attack.

And yet, they are not altogether defenceless. Some species secrete from skin glands waxy filaments which cover them so well as to make them invisible and inaccessible to an attacker. Sometimes one can see them floating in the air, their small white flake-like cover being their only visible sign. Many other species carry two slender tube-like openings, called cornicles, on their dorsal segments from which they can expel a drop of sticky fluid containing waxy blood cells. This secretion will clog the mouth-parts of any assailant, who instead of biting the aphid will rather be kept busy cleaning himself. Moreover, it has been found that the secretion of the dorsal tubes contains an

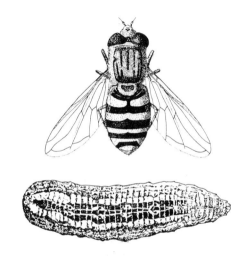

(*Top*) Hoverfly (*Syrphus*). Its markings are bright yellow.
(*Bottom*) Hoverfly larva—an avid exterminator of aphids.

"alarm substance" which by its smell seems to alert other aphids in the vicinity, inducing them to withdraw their proboscis and to flee the danger zone. Ill-equipped though they may be for a rapid get-away, they can resort to one method of escape and frequently do: they simply let themselves drop to the ground. Of course this is still a hazardous business, for the chances of their finding a way back to a suitable host plant or other feeding ground must be rated as extremely slender.

These defences, modest though they might be, together with their enormous powers of reproduction enable the aphids to hold their own against their predators and the hazards of their migrations. A balance

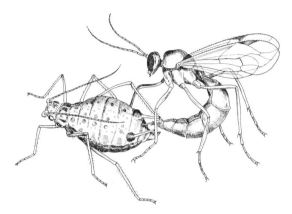

Small ichneumon fly of the species *Lapidus* depositing its egg in a plant-louse. The larva will parasitically live off the host and will literally eat it alive.

Corpse of an aphid. The parasitic larva has dug its way out and has pupated under it.

is established in this way between what is tolerable to the host plant and what ensures the survival of the aphids. This balance of nature is of paramount importance in the shared life of plants and animals, a balance seriously threatened mainly by man who—be it deliberately or unwittingly—often disturbs the natural state of affairs with most unwelcome consequences.

A historic case in point which occurred at the end of the last century in California may serve as an example. It was blossom time in the orange and lemon groves when a seemingly harmless parasite made its first appearance, having been brought into the country from Australia with some plants. This insect, the cottony-cushion scale (*Icerya purchasi*), a close relative of the aphids, multiplied so rapidly in its new habitat that the fruit trees withered and the future of the citrus growers seemed in jeopardy. In their despair they dispatched an entomologist to Australia to find out why this insect was so much less destructive on its home ground. His answer was that it was being kept in check by a natural foe, the vedelia beetle (*Rodolia cardinalis*), which unfortunately had not accompanied the cottony-cushion scale to California. Once the predator, too, had been imported to the USA, it promptly set to work and very soon citrus cultivation was back to normal.

The type of measure then used in California for the first time is called biological control. In employing the natural enemies of the pest, a specific weapon is being brought to bear. We have mentioned such a case when we discussed the fight against malaria where certain small fish can be introduced to prey on the larvae of the disease carrier (see pages 31-32). These methods are being continually improved and extended and have already proved their worth against over 100 different pests. By contrast, poisonous insecticides can affect beneficial as well as harmful insects and, via the food-chain, can kill fish, birds and mammals, as well as cause harm even to humans. Therefore, whenever chemical methods cannot be avoided, efforts are being made to use at least substances which are selective in their action. Consequently the use of broad-spectrum, persistent poisonous chemicals which might pass from one organism to another has now been banned. That means that DDT—once so highly thought of as an insecticide—has also had to be eliminated from the list of approved control substances.

What to do against aphids

If our rosebuds are shrivelling or cinerarias in their window-boxes wilting, most of us will hardly worry about the wider implications of the balance of Nature: we shall want to get rid of the particular pest as quickly as possible. A perfectly reasonable wish and one that can be met by the use of a sprayer. A number of effective preparations, tested under the official Agricultural Chemicals Approval Scheme, are available from gardening supplies and hardware shops and should be used as recommended by the manufacturer. Of the suitable chemicals, derris is non-persistent and, to the user, one of the least toxic substances. Aerosol dispensers are handy and always ready to use.

It may even be worth gently picking up the odd ladybird in the garden and, having carried it indoors on a sheet of paper or a paint brush, depositing it on one of the infested house plants. Given the right species of ladybird—the seven-spot kind, that is—it will probably set to work with a healthy appetite. In this way biological pest control may be practised and its effects studied in the home.

Wood ant (*Formica*) carrying a stone while building its nest.

Ants

About three-quarters of all known animals are insects and for variety of
shape and appearance they are unsurpassed in the animal kingdom.
But only a few groups of insects have managed to evolve a social
organization, i.e. bees, wasps, termites and ants. Bees produce honey—
that much at least everyone knows; the same applies to the painful sting
of the wasp. Termites, on the other hand, living in warmer climates, are
almost unknown in our country. As for ants, despite their universal
presence, they are not exactly popular, and if they happen to build their
nest on our favourite picnic spot or invade our house, they become a
nuisance. And yet they are remarkable creatures.

Of ants in general

In the history of our planet, the emergence of man as a social being is
a relatively young phenomenon dating back no further than 10,000

years. Yet ant colonies existed as long as 10 million years ago! Some of these insects, trapped and sealed in amber, the resinous gum which dripped from the trees, have been preserved in all their delicate detail. In the main they belong to species which are still extant. Others have come down to us as 100-million-year-old fossils dating from the Cretaceous Period, with the origins of their social organization going back even further. Nowadays people are seriously concerned about man's chances of survival in the next century should the population explosion continue. Obviously ants are far better at coping with changing conditions of life: they have managed to establish themselves in every corner of the earth, from woodlands, meadows and cultivated fields to steppes and even deserts, from the tropics to the wastes beyond the Arctic Circle. There is not the slightest indication that they need worry about their future.

Over 6000 ant species have so far been identified, some no more than one millimetre long, others, at the other extreme, with an overall length of 40 millimetres. Whereas most bees and wasps are solitary creatures—a fact not generally known—and some others represent intermediate stages in the evolutionary development from solitary to social life, ants are always social beings. Some ant colonies comprise hardly more than a dozen members, yet others number as many as 10 million inhabitants, comparable to the population of a metropolis. What about their family life, however?

The ant community

The head of every ant community is the queen. Generally there is but one in each colony and, as with the queen bee, being the only sexually fully-developed egg-laying female, she is the real focus of society. The overwhelming majority of the members of the colony consists of "worker ants", females with underdeveloped ovaries, unfit to propagate. They carry out all the tasks necessary for the continuance and well-being of the colony: they look after the queen and the young, build and maintain the nest, carry the food, defend the home and perform a number of other duties as well. In all these activities there is some division of labour and, allied to it, a certain diversity of physical shape. Not only do queens differ in looks from the workers, but the latter can vary in appearance within the same colony. On the simplest level, they might differ in size, the smallest as a rule working in the nest and the larger ones outside it. In addition to the ordinary workers, there exist in some species ants with large heads, strong mandibles and masticatory muscles, called "soldiers". Not necessarily more warlike than the rest, all they may be required to do is to crush and prepare hard food, such as seeds, while sitting peacefully at home. Other species, which build their nests in tree trunks, include specimens with enlarged heads fitting accurately into the entrance hole of the nest, so that these "doorkeepers" act as live plugs. Only members of the colony requesting admission will be allowed to pass. With a third species, three or more different types of workers may occur in a single nest, each with its own duties. So much for the diversity—the polymorphism—of the ant. The next question is: what about the males?

Males appear only at certain times of the year and are hatched from unfertilized eggs. If the queen fertilizes her eggs with the sperm cells from the special pouch she is carrying in her abdomen, the brood

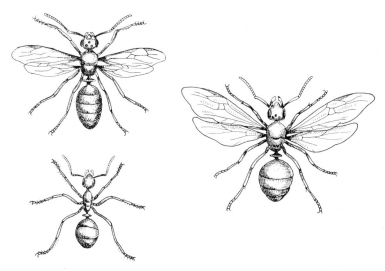

(*Right*) Young queen (fully developed female); (*Left top*) male;
(*Left bottom*) worker of red wood ant.

hatched will be females—a queen or workers; if the eggs stay unfertilized they produce males. This mode of determining the sex of the next generation is also present in bees.

Worker ants are always wingless, but what they lack in mobility they make up by industry. The sexual forms, i.e. males and queens at the start of their adult life, possess wings (figure on p. 101). The nuptial flight of a swarm of ants, say on a hillside on a fine, warm day, is quite a sight. As if by previous agreement, the young males and queens become suddenly very agitated in their nests, pour from their entrance holes in the ground into the open and rise into the air like a cloud of smoke. Usually they make for a prominent landmark near by, a hilltop for instance, there mingling with swarms from other colonies, thereby preventing inbreeding. During the flight and occasionally afterwards on the ground, queens and males come together. This may occur several times in succession, for the supplies of sperm cells the queen accumulates in her sperm pouch on this occasion will have to last her for the rest of her life and that can be 20 years or more. Thus, after a mating flight one queen was found to have stored 320 million sperm cells!

The vast number of insects involved in such mass flights may surprise the observer, but it is essential for the survival of the species seeing that the losses incurred are equally huge. To their enemies these winged ants are great delicacies; birds in particular and many insects, too, are constantly after them. As for the males, even if they escape their enemies, they have no further tasks to perform and die soon afterwards.

The fertilized queens now seek to found new colonies, albeit only a few of them will succeed. Their first concern after their return to earth is to shed their wings, being no longer of any use to them. They spread and press them to the ground, pushing and tugging at them with their legs until they break off at a preformed abscission line near the wing base. Thereupon the queen digs a small cavity in the ground, blocks the entrance from the inside and gets ready to spend the next few months immured in this prison of her own making. She lays a pile of eggs from which the first set of larvae will eventually emerge. As no outside source of food is available in this sealed chamber, the queen must draw on her own reserves, i.e. her body fat and powerful flight muscles which are now no longer required. These reserves are broken down and converted into a nutritious glandular secretion for the larvae. Occasionally the larvae's diet is supplemented by the odd egg or two, and the queen may even partake of one of her own eggs. After all, she could not possibly cope on her own if all the eggs were to hatch out. In fact, as a rule she gives preferential treatment to one or two selected larvae, feeding the rest just enough to keep them from starving. In this way only one or two larvae will at first be brought on (figure below). Only when this first batch has pupated does she turn her attention to the remainder. Meanwhile the initial "hand-reared" batch will have metamorphosed and have produced the first workers. Swinging into action at once, they open their dungeon, start foraging for food and building materials, and tend the larvae: a new colony has come into being. At the same time the queen, relieved of all her chores, now has but one function for the rest of her life—to lay eggs.

Queen (genus *Camponotus*) in her self-made cell tending her brood.

This is the procedure followed by the carpenter ant (*Camponotus*), the largest species found in our country, whose workers may attain 14 millimetres in length. That species prefers building its nest in partly decayed wood. The way ants establish their colonies, however, can be subject to many variations. Another example will illustrate how different methods can achieve the same aim.

In the case of the small red wood ant (*Formica polyctena*), which builds such tall anthills, the young fertilized females, the queens, will be welcomed back into their own nest or taken in by another colony of the same species. Here the queens are not hostile to each other and consequently dozens of them may share the same nest and lay their eggs there. The result is a tremendous growth in population, leading sometimes to the establishment of "branches" in the neighbourhood, i.e. new anthills connected with the mother-colony by permanent trails. These satellite establishments keep in touch with their nest of origin by an exchange of population and remain a part of the original colony. Equally, they can become fully independent entities with several queens, up to 100 metres distance from the original nest.

In contrast to the short-lived males, queens, as mentioned earlier, may live to a ripe old age. Workers can live up to three years if they escape all the hazards threatening them. Colonies with one queen will last her lifespan; those with several queens may survive for decades. One septuagenarian colony certainly showed no loss of social vigour whatever.

Ants as builders

Compared with the elaborate edifice constructed by the bee, the ant's efforts at homemaking seem poor. In its simplest form it consists of a vertical shaft in the ground with blind horizontal passages leading off it. The deepest chamber is reserved for the brood, those closer to the surface for use as storage and refuse dumps. Other species deposit excavated earth, together with material collected elsewhere, on top of the nest, which leads to the formation of an anthill. The nest's irregular passages and chambers extend deep underground (figure on p. 105), vegetation and roots reinforce the structure and this is further strengthened by the ants' secretions. In the chambers the workers tend the brood.

In time larvae emerge from the eggs as white grubs (figure on p. 106), a stage of development corresponding to the caterpillar of the butterfly. With most species these grubs spin a cocoon just before pupating (figure on p. 106)—the so-called "ants' eggs" which cage birds and goldfish consider such a treat. The genuine article could hardly satisfy their appetite.

A bee or wasp will spend its entire early life, i.e. until it emerges from the pupal stage, in the same cell of the comb. By contrast, the ant brood's accessibility and careful storage according to age has the advantage that it can be moved by the workers at any given moment to the part of the nest enjoying the most favourable conditions from the point of view of warmth and humidity. The effort involved in such continuous chopping and changing is substantial, particularly in the case of the wood ant (*Formica rufa* and *polyctena*) whose mound, built up of pine needles, twigs and scraps of moss, can grow to a height of several metres. The biological purpose of these huge mounds appears to

Cross-section through the nest of the common black ant (*Lasius niger*). The chambers extend far into the soil below the nest.

be to act as solar heat traps: the sides catch the rays of the low-lying morning and evening sun and are warmed at a time when the ambient temperature is low, while inside the workers are busy rearranging the brood to enable it to benefit from the warmth and to speed its development. But ants possess yet another means of affecting the temperature in the nest. In good weather they will quietly "sunbathe" in their thousands on top of the nest until their bodies are thoroughly warmed through. They then scurry below while others take their places, and, like living storage heaters, proceed to give off the accumulated

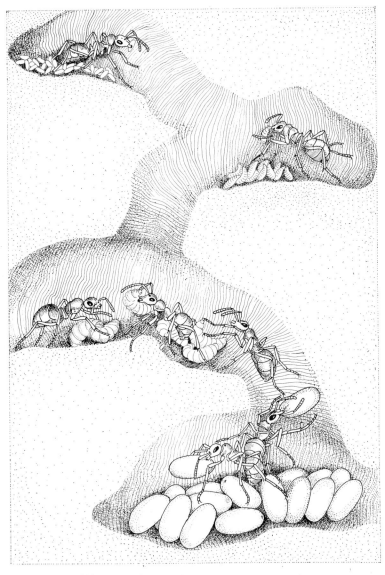

Detail from nest of the common black ant containing: (*Top left*)
eggs; (*centre*) larvae; (*bottom*) pupae.

warmth at the desired places. Finally, just as we close windows and doors to keep out the cold, so ants plug the numerous entrances to the heap with nesting material at nightfall or when the weather turns cold.

Only relatively few species of ants build underground or domed nests. Others inhabit rotting or even sound wood in which they tunnel their passages. Still others manufacture paper from which they create, say in a hollow tree trunk, "carton" nests. However varied their appearance might be, the internal lay-out of the nests is generally based on the same simple principle: a system of chambers and passages providing shelter and accommodation to the workers for their functional activities.

If anyone imagines that an ants' nest is just a loose association of individuals and not a tight-knit, well-organized community, let him try to disturb the closely regulated life of the colony. In the general commotion following such an upset, the workers will with lightning speed seize the exposed larvae and pupae and carry them in their mandibles to safety in the deeper layers of the nest. Others will

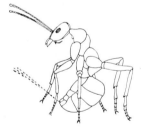

Red wood ant with non-functional sting directing
a spray of poison against an enemy.

promptly turn their weapon on the intruder. Many ant species possess a poisonous sting; in others the sting has degenerated and is no longer functional, so the poison is squirted at the enemy from the rear segments of the abdomen, which is aimed forward for this purpose (figure above). The formic acid sprayed in this way can be smelt on your hand if you beat the nest a number of times with your palm on a fine, warm day when the ants are active. Not all species of ants produce formic acid in their poison glands—differences exist here as well—but whatever the substance produced, it will always be a deadly poison to other small insects.

As soon as the cold weather sets in, the ants withdraw to the depths of their nest and go into a torpor until roused back to active life by the spring sunshine. Unlike bees, they do not hoard food for the winter and therefore can only survive the enforced fast by adopting this energy-saving state.

Feeding habits of the ants

On the whole ants lead a predatory life, their victims being mainly insects. Whenever during their foraging trips into the surroundings of their nest they come upon a bulky victim—say a caterpillar—they hurry back to the heap in great excitement, summon their nest-mates, and then return to the spot as fast as they can. During this return journey they lay a trail by frequently dabbing the ground with their scent gland in the rear end of the abdomen. The alerted ants follow this trail and soon the caterpillar will be surrounded by dozens of ants, all mercilessly directing their poisonous sprays at the victim. Eventually it will succumb to this attack, though now and again it may still be alive and struggling while being dragged to the nest in a concerted effort. The scent also helps the ants to find their way back to the nest, but they can use other navigational aids, e.g. the sun, whose position they have noted on their outward journey, as well as landmarks along the route. Once safely in the nest, the booty is cut up and processed.

The ants' enormous food requirements may at times be even of economic importance. For instance, the red wood ant (*Formica polyctena*) with its huge domed nests becomes the forestry workers' welcome ally whenever trees are threatened by insect pests. In an evergreen forest badly infested with web-spinning sawfly it was found, for example, that every day between 1000 and 10,000 sawfly larvae were being brought into a single nest by the 200,000-odd worker ants. Wood ants have therefore become "protected" insects and the collection of their "eggs" has been banned—to the regret of all bird and fish fanciers.

Many ant species, on the other hand, are plant-feeders with a marked liking for honeydew, the sugary substance which, as mentioned in the previous chapter, aphids extract from the plants and excrete as being surplus to their requirements. Thus when an aphid excretes a

Ant (*Tetramorium caespitum*) stroking with its antennae a sucking aphid, thereby inducing it to release a droplet of honeydew.

drop of honeydew from its hind-gut, flicking it some distance so as not to "mess itself", the sugary fluid is eagerly collected by bees and wasps. Ants have developed a more intimate relationship with aphids. Certain ant species pay regular visits to colonies of aphids which oblige their visitors by not producing honeydew until actually requested by the ants to do so. The latter do this by stroking the aphid with their antennae, thereby inducing it to let a sweet droplet emerge from its anus which is adroitly caught by the ant. Some species of ants construct runs to tree trunks and up into their crowns along which hosts of workers can be seen marching to the aphid providers, returning with a crop full of honeydew after having "tanked up" at the top. An association for mutual benefit—symbiosis—has developed. The advantage of this arrangement to the ants is obvious; but the aphids, too, gain from it, if only in being left unharmed by these ferocious insect hunters. At times the benefit even includes special protective measures, e.g. earthworks built by the ants round and over the sucking aphids, forming, as it were, milking parlours for them, or their defence by the ants against predators.

Much more could be written about the feeding habits of the ants. Some are grain-collectors, depriving farms in certain countries of large portions of the cereal harvest; others are fungus cultivators, growing this food of theirs on special compost in underground plantations. But none of these species is native to our region.

Ants in the house and their control

Nobody likes to see his house invaded by ants. Whenever this happens, the offenders are usually the common black ants (*Lasius niger*) or the larger black-brown *Camponotus ligniperdus* or *C. herculaneus* which have been attracted by some sweet or other edible substance while out foraging. They are bound to return in greater strength unless something is done about them. In our country house on Lake St. Wolfgang the ants sometimes even beat us to the honey pot on our breakfast table, though as a rule they perish in the attempt, being unable with their full crops to negotiate the slippery inner wall of the pot. Occasionally they will make themselves at home indoors, building a nest under floorboards, behind the skirting or among logs of firewood.

As a result of the growth in communications, the native ant species may easily be joined these days by importations from abroad. The Argentine ant (*Iridomyrmex humilis*), for instance, has repeatedly appeared in Europe in this way. It is a most persistent nuisance, raiding domestic stores, stealing seeds from the vegetable patch and plundering bee hives, and having, on top of it all, a most unpleasant sting.

Another immigrant is the Pharaoh's ant (*Monomorium pharaonis*) which, hailing from tropical and subtropical zones, has also been spread all over the world by our modern means of transport. Unable to lead an open-air existence in our latitudes, these creatures establish their nests in congenially warm spots in our centrally-heated buildings and then take to roaming the place in long columns even in mid-winter. Only about 2 millimetres in length, or somewhat smaller than our smallest native open-air species, the Pharaoh's ant workers are recognizable by their amber-yellow colour and slightly darker hind part of their body. The queens, which are about twice the size of the workers, dispense with the nuptial flight and mate in the nest. Since each colony generally possesses several queens, eradication is difficult, for if but a single queen manages to survive, the whole effort will be wasted. These minute ants easily swarm from house to house along district-heating conduits and can infest whole streets, as happened in the city centre of Munich in 1975. Hospitals fear them particularly. Attracted by food, they will penetrate patients' lockers and can even gain access to wounds under dressings. As carriers of bacteria they present a serious danger.

Visitations by certain migratory ants found in Africa and America are of a special kind. The South American genus *Eciton* is a case in point. These "driver-ants" do not build nests but only bivouac for their short stop-overs by gathering in tight clusters in a cavity in the ground, with the queen and the brood safely protected in the centre. In times of food shortage camp is struck and moved several hundred metres every night; it is from these bases that the workers make their notorious raiding expeditions. Moving in massive columns through the surrounding countryside, they attack and devour with their sharp jaws all animals not quick enough to escape. Whenever they approach a human dwelling, all the inhabitants can do is to pack up and leave. Yet even this visitation can have its welcome aspect, for, to be sure, after these hordes have left no other insect will be left alive in the house.

Whereas such migratory ants will leave the house as quickly as they have arrived having completed their campaign of extermination, our native ants tend to establish themselves as permanent tenants. Their stings may not be dangerous but they are nonetheless unwelcome in the extreme. As a first measure against them it is advisable to keep all food that might attract them in ant-proof containers, admittedly not always easy to do in view of the smallness of the insects and their ingenuity in discovering entry points. A simple way of making a pot of jam inaccessible to them is to stand it in a larger bowl of water, for ants cannot swim. After a few days or weeks of unsuccessful search, the scouting parties will simply pack up and go.

Should direct action against them become necessary, say because they are found entering the house along certain runs, a number of very effective proprietary ant killers are now on the market. The best are a chlordane emulsion concentrate or bendiocarb water dispersible powder which should be applied according to the makers' instructions to areas around the points of entry. Ants' nests can be treated with lindane dust. The Pharaoh's ant, so difficult to control in the past, can now also be effectively tackled with dieldrin, chlordane or bendiocarb-based preparations.*

*For details of recommended control measures see Advisory Leaflet 366, Ministry of Agriculture, Fisheries and Food (Publications), Tolcarne Drive, Pinner, Middlesex HA5 2DT.

Silver-fish

Generally we do not notice these little insects, but if we lift up a flower-pot or shift a bag in the larder or open a drawer, we sometimes get a glimpse of a shining, silvery creature about one centimetre long darting hither and thither in terror, making desperately for the nearest cover. Its efforts to escape are sometimes cut short by a well-directed blow from the hand of a housewife, she being on principle suspicious of the intentions of every living creature she comes across in the house. So it is not often that we have the opportunity of studying this little creature at leisure. Before we have had a chance to have a good look at it, it has either disappeared in a crack or been overtaken by fate and reduced to a shapeless stain similar to that left by a clothes-moth in the same circumstances. Perhaps we shall deal more leniently with the next specimen we find.

Primitive insects

The silver-fish (magnified about 4 times in the illustration above) belongs to the insect order, sharing its general characteristics—a segmented body, six legs, as well as other features which are revealed only by dissection. The two thread-like feelers on the head closely resemble those of the cockroach. The three filaments at the "tail", stretching backwards as if to protect the body from behind, are distinguishing features of the silver-fish, and we wonder why Nature has not more frequently equipped small, defenceless creatures with such a practical device. The insect probably got its name from the shining scales covering its abdomen; they remain as fine silver dust in our fingers when we have crushed one of these little creatures. Such scales, formed from the chitin of the skin, are not uncommon in insects. We find them on many beetles. The brilliant colouring of a butterfly's wing is produced by the delicate structure and colouring of tiny scales embedded in the surface—the reason why the lustre fades so quickly when the butterfly falls into the inexperienced hands of young people.

In the case of the silver-fish, only the abdomen is covered with scales, for it has no wings at all. None at all, be it noted. The caterpillar of the moth and the maggot of the fly have no wings, but they develop in the pupal stage and the fully grown insect makes use of them. Neither the flea nor the bug can fly, but it is certain that their remote ancestors could fly very well and that the wings have only degenerated in consequence of these insects' parasitical way of life, a fact which is confirmed by the vestigial wings possessed by mature bugs today. There is not the slightest indication that the ancestors of the silver-fish ever were winged. The absence of wings, therefore, is considered to be an ancestral or primitive characteristic. Along with a group of cousins of various types, the silver-fish brings us, as it were, a message from the distant past.

While other insects were passing through all the preliminary stages before emerging as accomplished fliers, this little community simply stood aside and took no part in these developments. That was very long before the first human beings appeared on the earth. Other characteristics, too, point to the ancient lineage of these insects. That is why, insignificant though they seem, they have been singled out by the zoologist for special attention and why they are called "primitive insects", although no doubt they, too, have changed in many ways since the birth of the insect family.

A harmless housemate

The scientific name of our silver-fish is *Lepisma saccharina*—the sugar guest—an official confirmation of its sweet tooth. And not without reason, seeing that sugar is one of its favourite foods. It is not fastidious, however, and is also content with all kinds of animal and vegetable waste. The quantities it consumes are so trifling that it causes no damage to speak of, provided exceptionally favourable circumstances do not allow it to multiply too much. As it requires a certain amount of moisture, it does not thrive in dry rooms. The love of moisture is here, as in many other cases, associated with an antipathy to light. That explains why we do not notice these little housemates during the daytime unless they are accidentally exposed. They lay their eggs in cracks and abandon them to their fate. From the very beginning the young resemble their parents in appearance and have the same habits. The housewife need have no sleepless nights on their account: they take about a year to reach maturity and so do not multiply at the same rate as other pests. On the whole they are entirely harmless housemates.

Control

If the silver-fish are left undisturbed for a longish time in favourable circumstances, say in damp rooms which are little used and not thoroughly cleaned, they sometimes multiply to an extent that demands the employment of drastic measures of control. As they are also fond of dried paste or glue they may be a nuisance if present in sufficient numbers, since they will attack starched linen or curtains and damage book-bindings. They have even been known to gnaw through woollen material and leather.

It is not difficult to get rid of them if the rooms are well cleaned and aired. Spraying their haunts with a synergized pyrethrum (see footnote on p. 32) insecticide or dusting with carbaryl powder is also recommended.

A glance at the relatives of the silver-fish

Only a few species of this primitive insect become our housemates. Most of them live in the open air, little known and hardly noticed.

There is, for instance, one insect so like the silver-fish that the casual observer might well mistake it for one. Its habits, however, are entirely different from those of its cousin, who loves darkness and the four walls of a house, for it can be seen lying on a bare rock by anyone out for a walk in the hills.

Another relative lives as a housemate of ants. This "ant silver-fish" has shown considerable perspicuity and has hit on the right place for getting through life without worrying about its daily bread. For such an ant household is never short of stores. There are hundreds of thousands of inmates and they must all be fed. The innumerable insects that have been dragged inside provide an abundance of fresh meat, and there are sweets in plenty—honey and other delicacies. There are, in fact, quite a number of "guests" who make a habit of sharing the ants' stores. They have not been invited, of course, but the ants just have to put up with them.

Some of these gate-crashers are so small that they pass unnoticed. Others are literally so thick-skinned that the sharp jaws of the rightful owners of the house can make no impression on them. Others curry

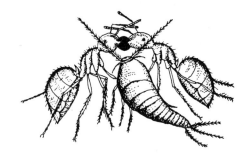

The ant silver-fish lives as a housemate of the ants and snatches the food from their mouths. (Magnified about 3 times.)

favour with their hosts and are given the run of the larder in return for the delicious scent and flavour of their secretions. They even go so far as to help themselves to the ants' eggs. The silver-fish guest is neither small compared with the ants, nor is it armoured, nor does it possess anything that could appeal to their senses. If an ant has had the luck to find honey and, in accordance with the habits of the species, has regurgitated it to share it with its fellows, the parasite creeps up from below and steals the sweet drop right out of the mouth of the expectorating member of the family (see illustration on p. 116). The thief then wisely beats a hurried retreat.

Another group of these primitive insects is not so good at running but all the better at jumping. For this it has a kind of spring fixed near the end of its tail and tucked under its abdomen when not in use (see illustration below); the spring can work downwards and backwards when required. With the help of this device the insect then takes a jump of which a flea might be proud. The goal is immaterial. The insect jumps at random; it is bound to land somewhere; it covers ground and in spite of the clumsiness of its legs it is thus able to reach a place of safety if danger threatens.

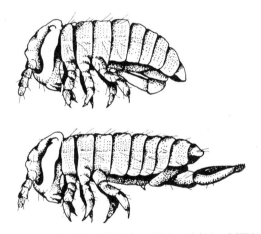

The water springtail. (Magnified about 50 times.) (*Above*) With tail flexed. (*Below*) With tail extended.

These springtails are minute insects, much smaller than the silver-fish. That is why they are usually unnoticed, although they are to be found everywhere. They live in moist earth and are frequent visitors not only our gardens but also in damp cellars and in flower-pots in rooms. Here innumerable members of a white species are often found whose jumping organs have atrophied, so that, like many other inhabitants of this earth, they can only make progress by crawling. A black species, often found on the banks of stagnant water, can multiply to such an extent that the ground looks as if it had been strewn with gunpowder. It is only when such a black speck is put under the microscope that we see its comical shape and its "spring tail" tucked under its body, which enables it to jump long distances. Another species inhabits snow-fields in the vicinity of glaciers. Observant mountaineers are often astonished to find this "glacier flea" and wonder what it lives on. They forget that such a tiny speck of life needs only the minimum of provender and can make do with grains of pollen and other organic dust that is swept even on to remote glaciers in more than adequate quantities.

Thus these little inhabitants of the earth can be found in the most remote and obscure spots, availing themselves of whatever slender means of subsistence even these may provide. We shall not begrudge them the one they may have chanced upon in the soil of our own flower-pots.

The house spider (*Tegenaria domestica*).

Spiders

Women detest spiders, whereas men for the most part regard them with indifference. They deserve neither our hostility nor our indifference. They do us no harm. On the contrary, they rid us of many troublesome and dangerous insects; and they are among the most interesting of all the animals that make their homes in our more immediate surroundings. It is true that a house with cobwebs in every corner looks neglected, and we can't blame the housewife if she feels obliged to sweep them away. But must every web in front of a window, on the verandah or in the summer-house be destroyed, and its maker killed?

Some say they are cruel creatures. How dreadful it must be for a fly to be swallowed alive! I don't know whether it is more painful to die in a spider's web or inside a swallow or in the treacherous toils of the fly-mould (p. 18). It is doubtful whether insects feel pain at all as we do. When a cockroach has hurt its leg during a moult, it is fond of licking its own blood; sometimes it does not stop at the blood, for it has been seen having a mouthful of its own flesh—a self-devouring cannibal! If you take a pair of sharp scissors and cut a bee in two, taking care not to disturb it while it is taking a drop of sugary water, it will go on eating. Its pleasure—if it feels any—is even considerably prolonged; it cannot drink its fill, for what it sucks trickles out again at the rear, and hence it can feast on the sweetness for a long time before it finally sinks dead of exhaustion. The story of Münchhausen's horse, which was anything but dead although a portcullis had cut off its hind-quarters, might be not fiction in the insect kingdom, but sober fact. Observations like the above do not support the view that insects have an acute sense of pain. To be sorry for a bird in the claws of a cat is understandable and justified, but only a sentimentalist will be sorry for a fly caught in a spider's web. So let us tolerate spiders, at least as far as domestic orderliness will allow. Let us watch them for a little.

Of spiders in general

Spiders do not belong to the insect order; spiders and insects are two related, but quite distinct, classes of animals. Along with millipedes and crustaceans, spiders belong to the group of invertebrates known as Arthropoda, which is divided into four classes. Of these, only the insects are the happy possessors of wings. Since, however, there are also wingless insects, such as the flea, the louse and the silver-fish, with which we are already acquainted, the absence of wings is not an infallible distinguishing feature. The number of legs, on the other hand, does show whether we are dealing with an insect or a spider: insects have six legs, whereas spiders have eight.

There is naturally no need to count wings in order to tell a garden spider from a dung-beetle, but there are spiders of all kinds and shapes, some 30,000 different species having been described. That is few in comparison with the one million or so of different insect species which have been classified by naturalists. Nevertheless, there are too many spiders for us to be familiar with them all, and that is why the expert also counts legs before pronouncing his verdict.

This is true in particular of the mites, often very tiny creatures, which are classified with spiders in the wider sense. More like the usual idea of a spider is the daddy-long-legs, whose body rests on eight horribly long, spindly, jointed legs. When they come strutting over the table or the floor, they must often enough pay for their alarming appearance with their lives, though they are actually quite harmless creatures, which live on dead insects and decaying vegetable matter.

The true spider has big silk-producing glands at the end of the abdomen (see illustration below). They exude a silk which hardens in the air and which we know from their webs. Many insects, too, have silk glands; they spit the thread from their mouths, as anyone knows who has ever watched a caterpillar making its cocoon. In the case of the spider, the glands have ducts leading to teats, known as spinnerets, situated near the end of the abdomen.

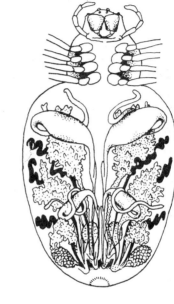

Garden or cross spider seen from below; on the underside of the head, the sharp fangs (jaws). On the thorax, the buds of the legs. Only the big silk-producing glands are shown in the sketch of the abdomen. They vary in structure and produce several kinds of silk, the quality varying according to the purpose for which it is used (cf. note on p. 123).

They use their thread for various purposes: not all of them make webs from it. The little jumping-spiders are freelance predators, not bound to webs. They can often be seen in grass, on roof beams, and on walls, now lurking in wait for prey, now hurrying a few steps forwards using their eight small, but well-developed eyes to spot a fly, on which they pounce with a bold and well-directed jump. The jumping spider kills its victim with its poison fangs and eats it up without more ado. A loosely woven nest gives it shelter at night; it is in this that later on it lays its eggs and keeps watch over them. The big wolf spider also roams at large in search of prey. Many of them can be seen running over the stones at the edge of our lakes and rivers. They weave a cocoon for their eggs and carry it about with them, defending it when necessary. As soon as the young spiders leave their silken cradle under their mother's belly, they crawl up on to her back. They ride along on her, thus enjoying her protection for some time.

Hind end of spider's abdomen with spinnerets (S). Abdomen opened to show part of the silk glands (G).

The six spinnerets are transformed vestigial legs. The silk glands terminate in the many pores on the spinnerets.

Crab spiders take it easy. "Arms" outstretched, they take up their position on flowers, and wait motionless for their prey. If an insect comes flying along to feed on the nectar, it is caught in a trice; instead of having the nectar in its mouth, it gets the spider's deadly injection in the back of its neck. Such spiders even attack bees and butterflies, opponents far bigger than themselves. Many use their thread to weave a silk roof to serve as a shelter in bad weather, strengthening it and filling in the gaps by working leaves into it. Faithful as adult crab spiders are to their quarters, they are equally fond of roaming in their early youth. Even then they do not exert themselves very much; they seem to be indolent by nature. If a clear autumn day gives promise of an undisturbed journey the young spider finds a high place either on a paling or on the top of a blade of grass. It hoists its hind end as high into the air as possible, and shoots out its silk. Suddenly all eight legs let go of their foothold and grasp the floating thread; the gentlest breeze wafts the little parachutist over considerable distances.

As there are many young spiders in late summer and as many other kinds use the same inexpensive means of transport, these drifting spiders' webs are a common sight in autumn. They are always associated with what we call an "Indian" summer. The most remarkable use the spider makes of its silk thread, however, is displayed in her crafty trap. Two different species of spider that make absolutely different webs often live with us as our housemates—the garden or cross spider and the house spider.

The spider in her web

A garden spider uses its web both as a parlour and as a trap. Woven entirely of silk it is, according to our standards, a very elegant parlour. The spider, on the other hand, who manufactures this material herself, does not regard it as either elegant or costly. Anyone who has ever noticed the great number of pores where the silk glands terminate at the end of a spider's abdomen (see figure on p. 121) will realize that she need never fear a shortage of silk, which is a blessing since it is essential to her life.

The web must be sticky if it is to catch flies. Yet the spider does not want to stick fast herself when she sits in her parlour or hurries over the strands, any more than we should appreciate having fly-papers strewn all over our floor. The dual purpose of the web is achieved by the use of two different threads: the centre, the spider's home, where she generally spends the day, is a network of dry threads. From this look-out rays of thread, also dry, are flung out as spokes to the outer rim. The web proper, between centre and circumference, is woven of sticky threads of silk produced by special glands,* the ends of which are made fast to the spokes. When the spider runs over the web, she uses

---

* The sticky silk is produced by the three pairs of silk-producing glands which are coloured grey in the figure on p. 121. The threads of the dry framework of the web come from the two pairs of big, bottle-shaped glands, the front pair of which extends to the spider's thorax. Secretions from special small glands near the spinnerets strengthen the places where the supporting and cross threads are attached to twigs and other objects. Three pairs of spiral, tubular glands, whose ends can be seen in the figure at the side of the big glands, produce the strong thread for the egg-cocoon.

the dry spokes and carefully avoids touching the sticky threads with her legs. In doing so, she is aided by two devices: at the ends of her feet there is an ingenious arrangement of hooks, toothed claws and bristles to hold on to the thin threads; then, if you look carefully you will see that the web is not vertical but somewhat slanting: the spider sits on the under-side and moves along upside down, which makes it easier for her to avoid coming into contact with the sticky threads.

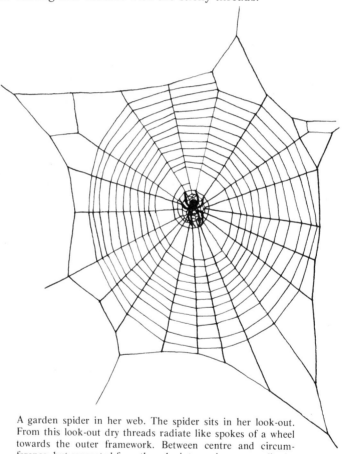

A garden spider in her web. The spider sits in her look-out. From this look-out dry threads radiate like spokes of a wheel towards the outer framework. Between centre and circumference, but separated from these by intervening spaces, lie the sticky spirals of the trap. (Reduced in size.)

Sometimes the garden spider sits in wait not at the hub of the web but at the rim, where she often weaves a kind of shelter of leaves. But there, too, she literally maintains contact with her web, as she doesn't want to miss the moment when any prey enters the web. So when she has taken up quarters at the rim, she always keeps a forefoot lightly poised on one of the spokes, sometimes also on a specially constructed "telephone" thread. As long as it does not vibrate she can sleep in peace.

The end of a garden spider's foot, with hooks and toothed claws and bristles. (Magnified about 100 times.)

The catch

It may sound strange to say that a garden spider relies on her sense of touch to inform her when a fly right in front of her eight eyes is entering her web. Yet it is true. Her organs of sight are poorer than those of the jumping spider. She can probably distinguish where light comes from and she also uses her eyes to get about in her own familiar little domain; but however hungry she may be she is not aware of a fly dangling in front of her if it does not touch the web. Her eyes are incapable of recognizing it.

We humans speak of what a thing looks like. For us, sight is the most important, the guiding sense. It is only the blind who are able to make a subtler use of our inborn sense of touch; those poor people who are born blind and deaf, like the celebrated Helen Keller, learn to develop their sense of touch to an extraordinary degree of keenness. Web-weaving spiders have used their sense of touch from time immemorial. If they could speak, they would talk perhaps of how an insect vibrates, rather than of what it looks like.

It requires not a little imagination to understand the make-up of a creature which learns by its sense of touch almost everything of importance to it. It is the vibration of the threads that betrays the presence of prey in the web. The strain on the web, which is indicated

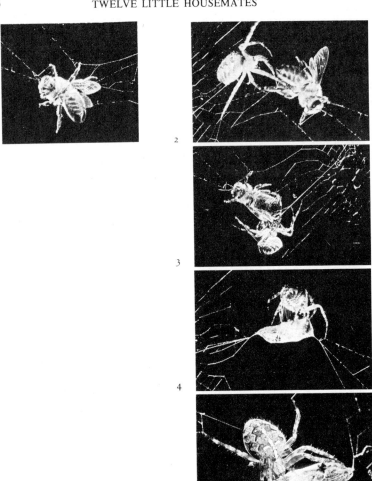

1. Honey bee caught in the garden spider's web has torn several
   threads.
2. Spider rushes from its look-out to the prey.
3. Spider begins to roll the bee round with its legs.
4. Bee is completely enveloped in a shower of fresh threads.
5. Spider kills the now defenceless prey with a poisonous bite.

by the tension of the spokes, shows whether the catch is plump or scraggy. The exact spot where it is hanging is also conveyed by the sense of touch. If the prey does not move, the spider plucks every thread in turn till she detects the right one. She finds her way to it immediately, for she is a genius in following up clues.

When a fly has got caught in a web, the first thing the spider does is to rush out and secure her prey. Even though the sticky threads make escape difficult, the attempts of some of the stronger insects are sometimes successful—provided the spider doesn't overtake them. If she does, she immediately envelops her victim in a shower of fresh threads, with the help of her deft legs—rolling it round and round so rapidly that it is enmeshed in no time and is soon absolutely helpless and defenceless. During these operations she bites it a few times with her sharp upper jaws, which are connected with poison glands. The poison in them is so lethal that a fly dies of its effects in a few minutes. The threads of the web are then bitten through and the parcel of food is ready for transport to the look-out, where it is immediately hung up by a short thread. Then the efficient spider has her jaws and legs free to deal with any fresh fly that might get into the web. If this does not happen, the spider settles down to enjoy her meal.

Now the spider's conduct is somewhat odd. It is as if we, instead of taking the top off a boiled egg and eating it with a spoon, were first only to bite it and, after spitting a little gastric juice into it, wait for the contents of the egg to dissolve and liquefy before we sucked it up. This is exactly what the spider does with the fly: she bites it, spits gastric juice into it and sucks up the dissolved contents together with the digestive juices. This process of spitting and sucking is repeated for some time and the persevering spider manages to imbibe all the dissolved muscles and intestines of the fly in a few hours. Only indigestible remnants of chitin are left and they are ultimately thrown out of the web.

If the spider has had a good day and has caught more flies than she can eat at the moment, the trussed game is hung up in the web as in a well-stocked larder. She scarcely ever grants an insect a reprieve and allows it to escape because her immediate needs are satisfied. On the other hand, if an enormous bluebottle or any other boisterous insect gets caught, the spider's anxiety for the safety of her web may prove stronger than her lust for prey, and with a few quick tugs she tears the entangling threads and lets the booty fall. The web will then be only slightly damaged, not completely destroyed.

Fooling a spider

About 400 B.C. there lived an artist in Greece called Zeuxis. The story goes that he was such a master of his brush that birds came flying to peck at the grapes he had painted. A spider would never have been fooled by any Zeuxis. However life-like his painted flies might be, they would mean nothing to her. But touch her web with a tuning-fork that has been struck and the vibrations of which approximate to those of a fly's wings, and out she rushes to bite it. If the tuning-fork is quickly withdrawn before she reaches it and a pellet of paper put at the spot where it touched the web, the spider falls on it. The deception does not go so far, however, that she is induced to eat the paper. After a brief investigation she tears the threads it is hanging by and the indigestible "prey" is flung out. How does she spot her mistake?

It is not the light weight of the supposed prey that deceived her, for if a tiny ball of clay is wrapped in the pellet, the spider reacts in the same way. And it makes no difference if the pellet is moistened with water. On the other hand, if the pellet is soaked in a kind of meat extract prepared from steeping a squashed fly in water, the spider bites it as if it were a fly, poisons it, trusses it up with silk and carries it off to her nest, where she will spend hours trying to suck her strange booty dry. Such conduct may appear "stupid". But who can blame anyone for being stupid if his senses tell him he is acting rightly? This neat experiment only shows us that not only the sense of touch but also the sense of taste plays an important part in the spider's life and that she trusts it implicitly.

Another experiment, as simple as it is illuminating, has shown that the garden spider can lay claim to a modest measure of mental activity, at least to some kind of memory. Suppose a spider is sitting in her lair at the edge of her web. A fly gets entangled, is caught, bitten, trussed and carried to the look-out and hung up there. During the short interval when the spider is getting ready for a good meal, a mischievous onlooker carefully cuts the threads by which the booty is suspended and the fly falls unnoticed to the ground. A dull-witted creature would simply accept the fact that the booty has disappeared. Not so the spider. She immediately begins to search her web patiently and systematically. One after the other she plucks and pulls at the spokes radiating from her nest. As they all sound alike, she runs to her shelter at the edge, half a metre away. Could she have hung the prey there and then have forgotten about it? When the search proves fruitless, back she runs to the look-out and plucks at the spokes again, and even runs to the spot near the edge of the web where the fly was caught. It is only after an inspection there and further plucking yields no results that she calms down. She settles to wait for a fresh victim, herself a victim of the naturalist's curiosity, cheated of the good cheer which should have been hers by right, since she had obeyed all the laws of the instinctive art of dealing with her prey.

How a spider's web is made

The spider's masterpiece is her web. If she had learnt how to make it at a school for weaving or from her parents, we should have to take off our hats to her. In reality she is born with a perfect mastery of her art and it is to Nature that we must pay homage for having produced a creature so perfectly endowed with such accomplishments.

Let us take as an example the web of the garden spider, since it is fairly easy to watch its construction. We must of course be up betimes, for she starts work early. As a rule she makes a new web in the early hours of every day or every other day, the old one having been spoiled by dust, insects or leaves entangled in it, or by other wear and tear. It is only the outer framework that lasts longer. Let us assume, however, that a completely new web is to be fashioned. How does the spider manage to fix the first thread where she wants it?

The conical spinnerets that we have already heard about (see figure on p. 122), and which send out silk threads from the tiniest of taps, are in fact vestiges of rudimentary legs and capable of movement. Suppose a garden spider on a tree trunk is about to start on a new web. She lifts her abdomen high into the air, shoots out some silk, stretching the spinnerets away from each other so that the silk forms a sail made of little tufts of thread, light enough to be borne away by the gentlest breeze. Thereupon the spider shifts her spinnerets to make them incline towards each other so that the silk threads that now emerge are combined into a single strand. This thread, sail in front, may float through the air for a distance of perhaps one or two metres. If this is all that happens, the spider hauls it back and eats it, and then tries her luck with another. If this one happens to come in contact with something solid such as a twig, it sticks to it. Then the spider makes her end secure, thus constructing her first bridge, which she immediately

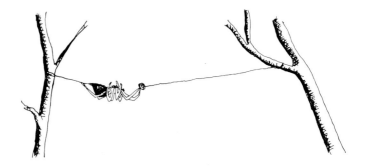

I: The bridge. So as to have a clear picture, the figure of the spider in this and the following illustrations has been enlarged. (Figures I-IX show how the web is made.)

proceeds to cross, doing so in a very odd fashion: she bites the thread through, but keeps hold of the two ends with her fore and hind legs, her body hanging like a bridge between them: she runs forward, shooting out fresh silk all the time behind her and winding up the thread ahead of her on her forelegs. As she pays out more thread behind than she winds up in front, the thread is lengthened so that the bridge sags. When she is midway she sticks the ends together and lets herself down to the ground. On landing she steps a little to one side (in Fig. II towards the spectator or away from him) and then fastens the thread to the ground. Thus the first three spokes are finished and the few steps to one side have ensured the slanting position of the web, which, as we noted before (p. 124), is all important for the spider's movements later, when the web is finished.

The next step is the construction of the first part of the framework. Now we must watch very carefully if we want to see how this is done. The spider has again climbed up to M, the centre of the future web (Fig. III). From M she runs to A and as she pays out a thread all the time, this spoke is now double. Back she runs along the double thread, still paying out, so that there are now three strands. After reaching a certain point—about at B—she suddenly does something surprising, but we immediately see why: at B she fastens the new (third) thread to

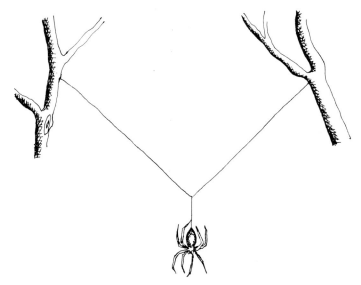

II: The elongated thread of the bridge is fastened to the ground.

the second one: running on past M to C, she reduces her output of silk, which tightens the new thread (Fig. IV) and thus pulls the second thread away from the first; thread number 3 is then fastened at C. In this way she makes a new spoke (B-M) and at the same time a part of the frame, though it is not quite satisfactory as it is over-taut and out of the perpendicular. To rectify this, the spider runs back to B and extends the thread of the spoke B-M, employing the same clever technique that we observed in the first stage of the construction: she

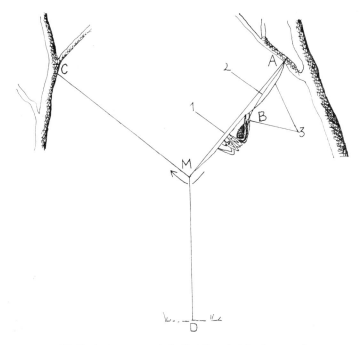

III: Preparing to stretch the first thread of the framework.

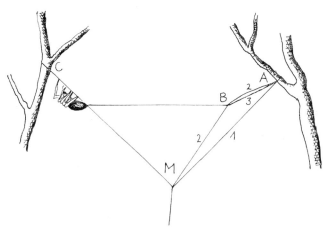

IV: The first thread of the framework (A-C) being tautened.

bites the thread through, bridges the two ends with her body and runs on to B, paying out more thread behind than she winds up in front (Fig. V). In this way she replaces the original spoke by a longer one, the outside thread (A-B-C), which, slack at first, is shortened and the dip at B is straightened out. This procedure is repeated: more outside threads are made, always in conjunction with a new spoke, e.g. outside thread C-D with spoke E-M, frame thread A-D with spoke F-M (Fig. VI). Now we can recognize the foundation of the web, though many more spokes have still to be added. To do this, the spider, starting from the centre, runs along one of the spokes, say M-E, to the circumference. She keeps

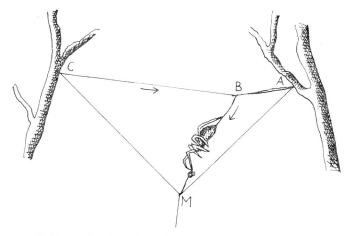

V: The outside thread is slackened, the temporary spoke B-M
replaced by the final one.

the new thread clear of the one already there, by guiding it with a hind leg and letting it roll over the claws of the foot as over a spool. When she has reached E, she fastens the new thread to the frame a little below E (at G in Fig. VIII).

In the present case the new spoke will be too slack, since G is nearer M than E is. But the spider hasn't finished yet! The spoke M-G is bitten through and replaced in the usual way, the spider's body forming a living suspension bridge between the two ends while she runs to M, paying out the permanent spoke behind and rolling up its predecessor before her. As the spokes appear, one after the other, they are fastened securely together at the centre by cross-threads and the future observation post begins to take shape.

The most important thing is still lacking: the sticky thread which is to trap the insects. In order to fix it, the spider must first make a temporary spiral, or scaffolding of dry thread. She runs from spoke to spoke, stretches her abdomen towards the circumference and, running round four or five times, fastens her silk thread to the spokes wherever

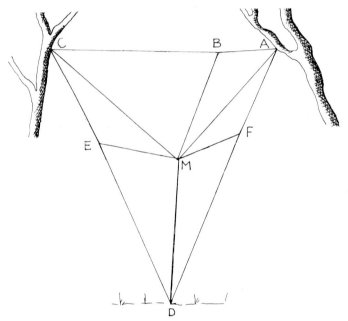

VI: Two more frame threads have been made along with two more spokes.

it crosses them. When she reaches the circumference she turns and now works in reverse, running towards the centre, making a much closer spiral of sticky thread between the widely spaced rounds of dry silk (Fig. IX). She uses the scaffolding of the first spiral both in order to get from one spoke to the next and as a guide for the sticky thread, much as a gardener keeps his rows of plants straight by first stretching a guiding thread across, thus keeping the main lines of his plan intact while he is filling in the details. As the sticky spiral grows, the temporary one, having served its purpose, is bitten out, rolled up and thrown away. At last the web is finished. Time, too, or our patience would have run out!

Naturalists are blessed with the gift of patience. They have watched spiders weaving their webs over and over again. All we have said is merely an introduction, for we have only described one particular way in which a garden spider might have made its web; it is astonishing how

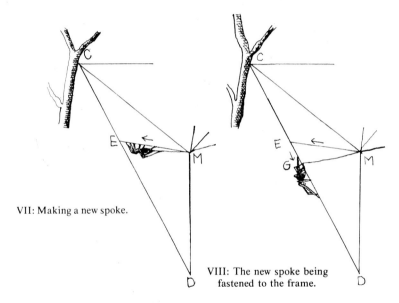

VII: Making a new spoke.

VIII: The new spoke being
fastened to the frame.

little the inborn skill of these animals is bound to a rigid system, how greatly their actions differ in detail according to local conditions and according to the weaver's character. If we were to start describing different webs of the various species of spiders, we should never stop.

My secret hope is that even this one example may induce many traditional enemies of the spider to watch one weaving her web if he ever gets an opportunity. The reader might then become an observer, the enemy even the friend of these amazing creatures, since hatred usually vanishes with increasing knowledge and understanding.

IX: The spider pays out the sticky spiral for trapping her prey, working from circumference to centre. What is left of the temporary spiral can be seen between the spider and the centre of the web. The framework has been omitted from this illustration.

A spider strums his serenade

In spring and early summer male garden spiders are not interested in females. They spin their own webs and lead independent lives until they have attained their maximum size, which is not saying much, because even then they are smaller than the buxom females. Indeed, the males of many species are mere dwarfs compared with their partners. In the spider world we certainly cannot refer to the females as the weaker sex. On fine days in late summer, the male leaves his web and goes roaming in search of a mate.

On such occasions every creature puts his best foot forward and makes the most of all his natural talents to impress the opposite sex. The peacock displays the glory of his tail, the blackbird pours forth its melody, while many butterflies emit an odour from special scent-producing glands which goes to the females' heads. What are male spiders to do? Their prospective partners cannot hear, their eyesight is poor, and they have little by way of a nose. So when the male spider goes courting, he concentrates on touch, the all-important sense in a spider's life. If he comes across a female's web in the course of his roaming, he attaches a strong thread to its edge from some suitable point in the neighbourhood and then plucks at it. The female in her parlour notices that the "telephone is ringing"; there must be an urgency in such vibrations, a special note of passionate desire communicated to the female's superfine sense of touch, for provided she is in the right mood, she immediately hurries to the thread and goes forth to meet her partner on the "bridge of love".

It is a dangerous job being a male spider. Should his visit be inopportune, it may end in his being seized and devoured right away by the bigger and stronger female. The same thing may happen even if the female submits to his advances though the end may be drawn out until she has had time to satisfy her sexual desires and her appetite for food. It is not uncommon for the garden spider to thus murder her mate once he has performed his function, and with other species it is the general rule. The male of some species is sufficiently diplomatic to offer the lady of his choice a trussed-up fly to dine on when he is approaching her, thus saving himself from being devoured.

Round about September the female garden spider lays her eggs, and deposits them in the soft, yellow cushion she has spun, which she keeps in a sheltered spot. Her life comes to an end with the first frosty night. In the following spring the young spiders hatch out of the eggs, exactly like their parents, only smaller. For some days nourishment is provided by the considerable supplies of yolk in their abdomens. Soon, however, they adopt the habits of the family and spend the summer catching and devouring prey. With autumn, the time comes for the males of this generation to sally forth to strum their serenades outside the webs of the females.

House spiders

The garden spider prefers to live out of doors, though she is not shy about entering our houses and often enough spins her web before our eyes. Where house spiders occur, and are tolerated, they are our housemates in the true sense of the word. Their traps are to be found in the corners of our living-rooms, in cellars, attics and summer-houses. Though these mat-shaped cobwebs, which sag slightly in the middle, have not the artistic finish of the orb webs of garden spiders, they serve their purpose fairly well. When a fly or midge is caught in a web, with its legs entangled in the mesh, it is promptly seized by the watching spider. She lies in wait in a tube woven in such a way that it is sheltered and leads into the bottom of the snare. The spider generally passes her time in this tube, emerging to catch game and disappearing into the tube with her prey in order to have a meal in peace and safety.

In contrast to most other spiders, who live only for one year, the

The web of a house spider.

house spider may live from five to seven years, unless of course her days are cut short by the housewife's broom. For the cobwebs at the corners of walls and ceilings are traps not only for flies but also for dust and dirt. They are not regarded as ornaments, and, moreover, there is another reason for their removal: spiders in living-rooms and bedrooms are often dreaded as poisonous. Are they really dangerous?

Are spiders poisonous?

Spiders certainly are poisonous. The duct of a poison gland perforates the sharp point of the spider's upper jaw, its secretion, which is injected into the wounds made by the spider's bite, causing the death of the trapped insects. But can spiders harm us with their poison? On the whole, no. The jaws of a garden spider or of a house spider are not strong enough to pierce our thick skin; nor are they constructed for this purpose. If they really do succeed in doing this where the skin is thin, the results are no worse than those following the bite of a midge. We need not worry: none of these spiders will hurt us seriously with their poison! So there is no point in our pursuing them as if they were dangerous animals.

Some other members of the spider family do not have such a blameless record. The bite of a water-spider found in our part of the world can smart unpleasantly. The Italian tarantula, a member of the wolf spider species, can also bite quite effectively, though the consequences are not grave. Medieval reports of people "bitten" by a tarantula and being driven to go on dancing till they collapse from exhaustion are, like many such rumours, just fairy tales. There is, however, a wolf spider in Brazil whose poison may cause a severe affection of the skin over a considerable area round the bite.

Really dangerous is another kind of spider, several species of which are found scattered over various parts of the world: in Italy and Southern France there is the "malmignatte", a spider that hunts grasshoppers, in Asia a near relative—the Black Wolf, and in tropical America the notorious Black Widow. The bites of such spiders are not only extremely painful, but may cause fever, amnesia and other disturbances and they may prove lethal. Of course none of these spiders deliberately attack men as prey. But it can happen only too easily that some person or other, who may be reaping or who may perhaps just chance to pick up some leaves, may inadvertently crush one of these spiders, which, feeling itself threatened, will then bite in self-defence.

In England Black Widows have repeatedly been kept in zoos, with the appropriate precautions. How greatly they are to be dreaded is shown by the fact that in critical times they functioned as a kind of political barometer. When there was a possibility of war and a bomb liberating them from captivity, these valuable creatures, the whole collection of them, acquired from such distant lands, were all destroyed. The risk of their running wild had to be prevented at all costs.

Spider's silk

More than 200 years ago a pair of gloves and a pair of stockings made of spider's silk were submitted to the French Academy of Science, but much earlier than this, spider's silk had been used for sewing in many parts of China. Although occasionally the services of our garden spider as a silk manufacturer have been required, the big, web-weaving spiders of tropical parts are far more profitable for this purpose. In Madagascar and in the tropical parts of East Africa there is a "silk spinner" whose web measures almost two metres across, and the legs of the mature female of this species are a good twelve centimetres round. In spite of its size, it supplies a thread 0.007 mm. thick, the finest natural silk that can be used in technical production. It is so fine that a length of it sufficient to go round the equator would not weigh as much as two kilograms. Other glands of the same spider produce a somewhat coarser thread which is also used by manufacturers. Spider's silk is as strong as the real silk produced by the silk-worm and is even more elastic. Material woven of spider's silk is extremely beautiful and durable. It would certainly have ousted real silk from the markets of the world if its production were not so costly. It is easy to breed silk-worms in great numbers, since they are content with a daily ration of leaves. Who would like to catch the flies necessary to keep a spider farm going? To save this time-consuming labour, either the egg cocoons are collected out of doors, or, alternately, adult females are caught and the thread drawn out of their bodies. Progressive factories have installed a simple, ingenious device for this purpose.

Spiders as suppliers of silk for man.

About two dozen spiders are installed in a frame, one beside the other, by laying the slender waist of each over a little board and keeping it in position by means of a wooden slide. There the defenceless creatures hang in rows while the thread, which sticks to the fingers, is "milked" from their spinnerets. All the strands are combined to form a single thread and this is fastened to a spool which slowly revolves until the supply of silk is exhausted. In this way about 300 metres of silk can be obtained at one operation. If the spiders are let out into the garden at intervals, the "milking" can be successfully repeated after a short time. The yield of one female from a series of "milkings" is a thread of about two kilometres long, quite a respectable output. The process, however, is much too complicated to make large-scale production worth while. Dresses of spider's silk will continue to be one of woman's unfulfilled dreams.

/

Ticks

With the exception of inveterate town-dwellers, most of us like strolling through the countryside and whiling away pleasant hours on the edge of a forest. Most likely, therefore, we shall have made the acquaintance of the wood-tick, unwelcome and clinging visitor that it is. In Europe it is the commonest and most widespread species of tick.

We know it in two very different forms, according to whether its belly is empty or full. If we notice a little brown disk crawling sedately on its eight legs over our skin, that is a hungry customer looking for board and a lodging to occupy for some time. After a few hours, if we leave it in peace, it will have bored its "beak" somewhere into our skin. It will stay there, sucking continuously till, after a few days, its shape will have changed beyond recognition: the blood it has imbibed will have swollen it into a bag the size of a pea (see figure on p. 143).

Spiders that do not spin

Ticks have to dispense with all the luxuries which the better-equipped true spiders can afford, thanks to their silk. They have no thread for trapping their prey, no silk cushion for their eggs, the males cannot court mates by "direct line", their young cannot launch themselves into the air by hang-glider, for none of them has silk-producing glands. Nevertheless, they are included in the same class as the spinning spiders since they have very much in common with them, including the number of legs.

The mites and ticks, the Acarina, are, therefore, an order of the Arachnida. This includes many species with differing habits: the itch-mite burrows in the skin of humans and other warm-blooded animals, the cheese-mite, as its name suggests, fancies other food, the flour-mite can cause damage to stored goods if it is allowed to multiply. Other species live as parasites of grasshoppers, butterflies and other

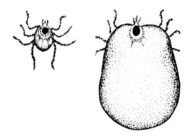

Wood-tick before a meal (*left*) and after (*right*). (Both figures magnified about 2½ times.)

insects, on whose bodies they appear as tiny, bright, red beads. Another species invades the breathing tubes of bees and can infest and destroy whole hives. Many other species might be added to this list; the observant will notice them in spite of their minute size, and often enough they will force themselves on the attention of the unobservant too, on account of the damage they cause. The great majority, however, pursue their hidden ways on land and in water without coming into contact with man.

The tick is the largest member of the tiny Acarina. Its unsegmented body has a movable head projecting from a kind of ruff; the biting and sucking parts stick out threateningly in front. The females are distinguished from the males by the many folds of their skin. Not that these are worn merely for show! They are strictly utilitarian, these folds of skin. The female sex is greedier and it is only the females who can take in so much blood that their bodies swell up into bags the size of peas. In two days their body weight can increase more than two-hundredfold. A human being would burst long before it had reached this stage. It is the folds in the female tick's skin that allow for expansion and thus make it possible for her to gorge herself without ill-effects.

Involuntary housemates

As there is good reason for the female's bloodthirstiness, we cannot blame her. Anyone who has to hatch out a few thousand eggs can do with a good meal.

As soon as the female has had her fill, she pulls her sucking mouth-parts out of the skin and drops to the ground. If this happens indoors, the consequences are anything but pleasant—for the tick. We may not be pleased when a slight irritation tells us we have got a tick, but the tick would be still less pleased if she knew what was coming. Nature did not intend them to be our housemates. It is unfortunate for them if they accidentally settle on our skin or—as more frequently happens—on a dog's skin, and thus get into a human habitation. They will continue to thrive as long as they stay on the skin and continue to suck, but once they fall off they will shrivel up very soon, instead of preparing for the next generation as every true mother does, consciously or unconsciously.

Ticks are not fastidious: in addition to humans and dogs, they will attack foxes, squirrels, hedgehogs and other mammals. In natural conditions, indeed, they settle far oftener on such wild animals as the latter than on a dog or human being, which is a blessing for the tick family, for in such cases the females, when they are engorged with blood, drop off from their involuntary hosts into the grass or moss in the forest, where they will find a suitable environment for the rest of their lives and where the future of their progeny is secure.

The tick's cycle of life

About a fortnight after she has dropped to the ground, the female starts laying her eggs, which she herself transfers to her head and back. After she has occupied herself thus for a few weeks, she begins gradually to shrivel up and, finally, hidden under some thousand eggs, she dies.

On hatching, the ticks have at first only six legs, which is surprising since they belong to the same order as the spiders. Actually, the last pair grows later, probably a matter of indifference to the lizards, snakes or young birds nesting on the ground whose blood is the first to be sucked. After sucking for a few days the tick drops off and moults. Now eight-legged and already somewhat bigger, they attach themselves to another lizard or snake. After a further moult they usually choose a mammal for their third and last meal. This sounds quite simple, but if we were tiny ticks, stationed somewhere in the grass or on the ground of the forest and had to wait for a lizard or, if we were older, for a fox or some other animal to pass our way before we could have a meal, I think we might have difficulty in summoning up sufficient courage to cope with life.

How the infant tick manages to find a lizard, I just don't know. Probably all it does is to wait until one crawls over it and then seize the opportunity. Many will wait in vain and starve to death. Owing to the combination of two circumstances ticks will not become extinct.

In the first place, they can fast for some time. Even the youngest of them can certainly wait a year for their first meal. One doubting naturalist cut his ticks' heads off to make sure they should not get a meal on the quiet. They lived in their headless state for four full years and even then they did not die a natural death. Actually, things do not happen like this. Of course there is not much chance of a lizard crawling today or tomorrow over a tiny speck in the grass. But one may come in the course of months, and if not this year, then perhaps next. And should some place prove so unfavourable that all waiting is in vain, the losses—if we forget the fate of the individual—are made good by the great number of progeny. It is, as we know, a natural law that animals with unfavourable prospects of survival are particularly fertile. One or other out of a thousand infant ticks will eventually come into contact with a lizard or snake after it has waited and fasted long enough.

Older specimens, who may feed on us as well as on other mammals, are more adventurous. They creep up tufts of grass and wait at the top of a blade for a suitable host to appear. Often they seem to occupy higher positions so that they can let themselves fall at the right moment. I have a vivid recollection of a rest we once took under the low shingle roof of an attractive memorial on Lake St. Wolfgang near Salzburg. When we set out again, we found we were covered with ticks. What betrayed our presence to them?

Animals with no sense of taste

Ticks have no eyes, so they cannot have seen us. The careful observer will detect for himself the sense they employ: he will notice that they sniff the air while they are perched high up waiting for a host.

Ticks, it is true, do not sniff in the way we do, for their organs of smell are located in little hollows near the "toes" of the first pair of legs. That explains why they sit with their forelegs raised, waving them slowly about in the air as soon as they are stimulated by a smell.

Another thing that helps them to find a host is their marked sense of warmth. If you put a few ticks on a piece of paper and hold a warm object several centimetres away from them, they will make a bee-line for it and follow the source of the warmth in whatever direction you choose to move it. After they have been enticed to some object with a good smell, perhaps to a piece of fresh fur, they immediately begin to wave their forelegs, which are lifted up like feelers while they are on the move, then halt and see to their moorings.

In their natural surroundings, too, they are apparently guided from their haunts to their prospective hosts both by the warmth emanating from the bodies of animals and men and by smell. In order to observe better how they feed, an attempt was once made to induce ticks to suck blood from a bottle covered by a membrane which was stretched over the top. When the blood was heated to the right temperature, they were attracted to it but did not suck. Probably their sense of smell told them something was wrong. When the ends of their legs, where the olfactory hollows are situated, were cut off they did go for the blood. As soon as there was no counter-signal from the "nose", the seductive warmth proved irresistible and they bored through the membrane and filled their stomachs with blood. Nor did it matter whether the bottle actually contained blood, for an enquiring person substituted soup, acetic acid and salt water: it made no difference to the ticks. They seem to have no taste. From time immemorial warmth and smell appear to have sufficed to guide them to the sources of food necessary for their survival. Creation's scheme did not provide for the tricks of scientists.

Ticks as disease carriers

Not only mammals but also birds are often plagued by ticks. The wood-tick we have been discussing is sometimes found during its youth on various birds as well as on lizards and snakes. Many other species live mainly or entirely on birds.

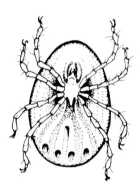

A pigeon tick, ventral surface. (Magnified about 6 times.)

One of these is the pigeon tick, which may occasionally be a housemate and a pest indoors. It belongs to a species of ticks which behave like bugs in that they attack their prey by night, returning to their retreat after a short meal of blood. Masses of them can be found in neglected dovecots. Great numbers have been found under flaking stones of the Votivkirche in Vienna and of St. Mark's in Venice or in other favourite haunts of pigeons. If they settle near houses they may become a great pest to human beings. An old house in Mainz was so badly infested that it was officially condemned and shut up. After nine months people thought the animals must have starved to death in the empty house. A new tenant, ignorant of the tick's record for fasting, had to pay for his ignorance with a long and serious illness, the prolonged fast having made these pests particularly vicious.

In warm countries, particularly in the Eastern Mediterranean area, a bird tick which is parasitic on hens, ducks, pigeons and geese, and which creates great havoc as the carrier of poultry diseases, is very common. Unfortunately these creatures are no respecters of persons and, given the chance, they will attack human beings as well as birds. They are known in Germany as "Persian bugs", a misnomer from the zoologist's point of view, for they are, and always will be, ticks. Yet the name shows that in that part of the world they are considered to be pests worthy of being ranked with bugs. So let us be content with our own wood-ticks.

In the past, man used to look upon the wood-tick as a harmless nuisance; recently, however, it was shown to be capable of carrying dangerous diseases. Thus ticks can transmit to humans—especially in springtime—certain viruses which cause meningitis, occasionally with fatal results (the so-called summer meningitis).

Protection from ticks

The wood tick is the species we have to contend with most frequently. Sometimes they can be noticed before they settle, since they often crawl about on us for hours before they find a soft spot on the skin. In that case all that is necessary is to kill them. This, however, is not so simple as with a gnat or mosquito. They cannot be swatted or crushed by force, for their bodies are incredibly hard and tough. Experts say it is better to set fire to them with a match.

Things are more difficult when they have already burrowed into the skin. They should not be simply pulled out, for the mouth-parts, with their hooks set at an angle, are so securely anchored that they are usually left behind in the skin when the body is removed and can then cause inflammation.

Fortunately the presence of the unbidden guest on our skin soon makes itself felt, for the spot begins to itch. If the tick is not yet very swollen, it can be covered with a bit of fresh sticking plaster. Next morning the tick will come away with the plaster when it is removed. It relinquishes its hold perhaps because it is irritated by the adhesive of the plaster and perhaps, too, because, being trapped under the plaster, it can get no air.

A method often recommended for extracting a tick is to bandage the bite with cotton wool soaked in paraffin. After some time the tick either withdraws its mouth-part voluntarily, or it can easily be pulled out. A drop of tincture of iodine will also generally induce the blood-sucker to let go, though if it has been feeding for some time and is swollen, this may take a few minutes. The added advantage of this method is that the iodine will disinfect the wound at the same time. Petrol, too, is reported to have been successfully used for tick removal.

Conclusion

Satisfaction is a rare feeling. People are always more concerned about what has been left out than what has been included. This applies to small as to large-scale enterprises, and it troubles me not a little. For many of our housemates have found no room in this book, very probably those on which information would be particularly welcome.

Someone has snails in his cellar and wants to know how to get rid of them. Someone else finds centipedes and wonders whether they are blood-sucking insects or whether they are neither blood-suckers nor insects at all. Another is plagued by the notorious death-watch beetle and a fourth by the cheese-mite. Many will complain that rats and mice have not been discussed and, finally, there are those who ask about dogs and cats, or about goldfish and canaries. The list of such wishes is endless. So perhaps I may be allowed to say a word to justify my selection.

This book is not meant to be either an encyclopedia or a textbook. All I intended was to give some information about a number of small housemates of ours whose names are quite familiar although little else is generally known about them. I also wanted to show that there is something wonderful about even the most detested and most despised of creatures.

> There's nought so humble, nought so small,
> But has a lesson for us all,
> The self-same magic everywhere,
> For eyes that see, and hearts that care,
> Riddles abundant, near and far
> From lowly flea to distant star.

Index